W9-BAN-025

Calligraphy
FOR KIDS

ELEANOR WINTERS

Sterling Publishing Co., Inc.
New York

Edited by Jeanette Green
Designed by Judy Morgan
Photos by Michael Hnatov Photography

Library of Congress Cataloging-in-Publication Data

Winters, Eleanor.
Calligraphy for kids / Eleanor Winters.
p. cm.
Includes index.
Contents: Calligraphy vocabulary—Tools and materials—Getting ready to write—Getting to know your pen—Italic calligraphy, lowercase (minuscule) letters—Italic calligraphy, capital letters—Gothic calligraphy, lowercase (minuscule) letters—Gothic calligraphy, capital letters—A new pen position—Uncial calligraphy—Roman calligraphy, lowercase (minuscule) letters—Roman calligraphy, capital letters—Numbers and punctuation—Writing a quote or a poem—Border designs—One-of-a-kind greeting cards—Copy machine greeting cards—Signs—Party invitations.
ISBN 1-40270-664-2
1. Calligraphy—Juvenile literature. [1. Calligraphy.] I. Title.
Z43 .W748 2004
745.6'1-dc22 2003023438

4 6 8 10 9 7 5 3

Published by Sterling Publishing Co., Inc.
387 Park Avenue South, New York, NY 10016

Distributed in Canada by Sterling Publishing
c/o Canadian Manda Group, 165 Dufferin Street
Toronto, Ontario, Canada M6K 3H6
Distributed in Great Britain and Europe by Chris Lloyd at Orca Book Services, Stanley House, Fleets Lane, Poole BH15 3AJ, England
Distributed in Australia by Capricorn Link (Australia) Pty. Ltd.
P.O. Box 704, Windsor, NSW 2756, Australia

Printed in China

Sterling ISBN 1-4027-0664-2

For information about custom edition, special sales, premium and corpoate purchases, please contact Sterling Special Sales Department at 800-805-5489 or specialsales@sterlingpub.com

For Leendert, with all my love
comme d'habitude

Acknowledgments

Calligraphy for Kids is in many ways a collaborative effort that resulted from the advice, encouragement, suggestions, and criticism of many friends and colleagues. All of them helped make this book possible.

Topping the list are my senior and junior consultants, Julia Paterson and Sarah Turbow, and my calligraphic partner and pal, Carole Maurer. Their experience and expertise have aided me enormously in organizing the book and its point of view. I am equally grateful to Heather Quinlan for her good advice and abundant enthusiasm; to Bob Cooperman for his instant rewrite abilities; Joan Harmon for all those pages of guide lines; John Golden for midnight-hour computer rescue missions; and Isabelle, our lovely and very helpful young model.

Special thanks go to my husband Leendert van der Pool for everything, everyday; to the Kitchen Girls, Kathryn Sartori, Laurie Sayres, Kathy Wallace, and again Julia Paterson; and to Terry Moriber for intelligent advice, unending encouragement, and good cheer. Finally, I'd like to thank Nan DeLuca and Carrie Robbins for pointing me in the right direction at the very beginning of this endeavor.

Thank you all!

Contents

PART I
Getting Started 5

1 ■ INTRODUCTION 6

2 ■ CALLIGRAPHY VOCABULARY 9

3 ■ TOOLS & MATERIALS 11

4 ■ GETTING READY TO WRITE 14

5 ■ GETTING TO KNOW YOUR PEN 17

PART II
The Alphabets 22

6 ■ ITALIC CALLIGRAPHY
Lowercase (Minuscule) Letters 23

7 ■ ITALIC CALLIGRAPHY
Capital Letters 36

8 ■ GOTHIC CALLIGRAPHY
Lowercase (Minuscule) Letters 48

9 ■ GOTHIC CALLIGRAPHY
Capital Letters 57

10 ■ UNCIAL CALLIGRAPHY 64

11 ■ ROMAN CALLIGRAPHY
Lowercase (Minuscule) Letters 73

12 ■ ROMAN CALLIGRAPHY
Capital Letters 80

13 ■ NUMBERS & PUNCTUATION 87

PART III
Using Your Calligraphy 91

14 ■ WRITING SMALLER 92

15 ■ BORDER DESIGNS 96

16 ■ GREETING CARDS 100

17 ■ PARTY INVITATIONS 112

What's Next? 116

Guide Lines 117

Index 128

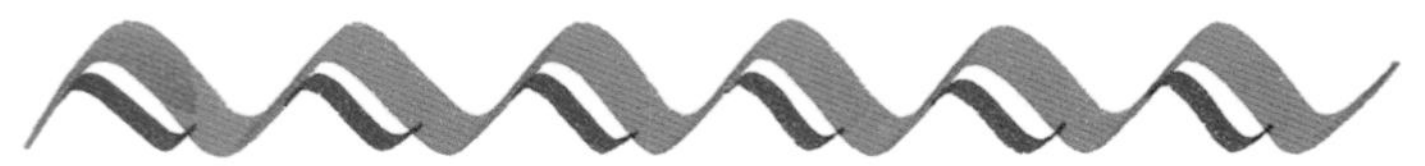

PART I

Getting Started

1

Introduction

Just a few years ago, it seemed as though no one could pronounce the word *calligraphy*, much less define it. Only a handful of artists were quietly keeping this age-old art alive. But all that has changed.

Today, nearly every art-supply store sells calligraphy pens, calligraphy markers, special paper, and dozens of books teaching you how to use them. There are lots of calligraphy classes in schools and craft shops all over the world. But most of these books and classes are for adults, and very little is offered especially for kids.

Now it's your turn. This book is for YOU.

There's no reason that kids can't learn to make beautiful letters, unless it's that you are all so busy! Kids can study and practice calligraphy with as much pleasure as painting or dancing or music. It is a skill and an art, but most of all, it's great fun! With a little effort and practice, anyone who can read and write can learn the art of beautiful writing.

But why should you learn calligraphy? Like any other art—drawing, painting, playing the piano—calligraphy helps you make your world more beautiful. A handmade birthday card, a poem written with beautiful letters, stationery printed with your name, or your friend's name hand-lettered in your own calligraphy, will make you feel good. And it makes a wonderful gift for your friends and family. It's an art (and a craft) that you can practice all alone on a quiet day, or with friends in a group, helping each other learn this fascinating art form.

WHAT IS CALLIGRAPHY?

Calligraphy means "beautiful writing" and refers to many other alphabets besides the ABCs we are all familiar with.

Thousands of years ago, Egyptians wrote with pictures called hieroglyphs. Chinese writing was also created from pictures that make up more than 40,000 characters. Chinese writing is much older than ours and has no alphabet. Other styles of writing, such as Hebrew and Arabic, have developed through the centuries, and all have their own alphabets and their own histories.

Some alphabets are no longer used, such as Mayan and Aztec, and exist only in ancient manuscripts that we can see in museums and art-history books. Other alphabets, like Greek, Arabic, Hebrew, and Russian, are used today as much as our own.

Our alphabet comes from the Roman Empire and is about 2,000 years old. For almost 1,500 of those 2,000 years, all writing was done by hand, which means that all books were done by hand—letter by letter, word by word. (You can imagine how long it took to make a copy of a book and how expensive it was!) For much of that time and even until the 1800s, people wrote with a quill pen, made of a feather, usually from a goose or a turkey. People sometimes also used wooden blocks carved by hand for printing words or pictures.

Until around 1200, most writing was done on papyrus, which is made from a plant, or on parchment or vellum, made from animal skin. Paper had been used in China for more than 1,000 years before it was used in Europe. After the invention of the modern printing press in the mid-1400s, paper was used because it was too difficult to print on parchment or vellum.

The printing press changed bookmaking considerably, but secretaries and other educated people continued to use calligraphy for writing letters, keeping records, and making important documents.

Today calligraphy is considered an art. Many people study it in special classes, mainly for the pleasure of making something beautiful. Calligraphers look at handwritten manuscripts and books from the past for inspiration and information. They continue a tradition that is an important part of our civilization.

LEARNING CALLIGRAPHY

Is it easy to learn? Well, yes and no. The instructions in this book have been written specially to make it as easy as possible for kids to get started. But like any other skill, you'll have to practice. In this book, we'll talk about ways to make your practice time fun and easy. But remember, you are the one holding the pen, and the more you practice, the easier it is to learn and the better your calligraphy will look.

This little book is going to cover a lot of ground. We're going to learn some basic facts about calligraphy and the different materials you can use. Then we'll try a variety of alphabets, learning how to make the letters and how to put them together to write words and sentences. In the second part of the book you'll find some projects that you can try, using your calligraphy.

A word of advice: Try not to do everything at once! It's easier to learn calligraphy step by step, rather than trying to swallow it whole. If you spend a little more time on the basics—which may seem very simple to you—the more advanced material will be much easier to learn.

Most of all, enjoy this book! We hope that you'll begin a wonderful experience and soon surprise yourself with the beautiful art that's right at your fingertips.

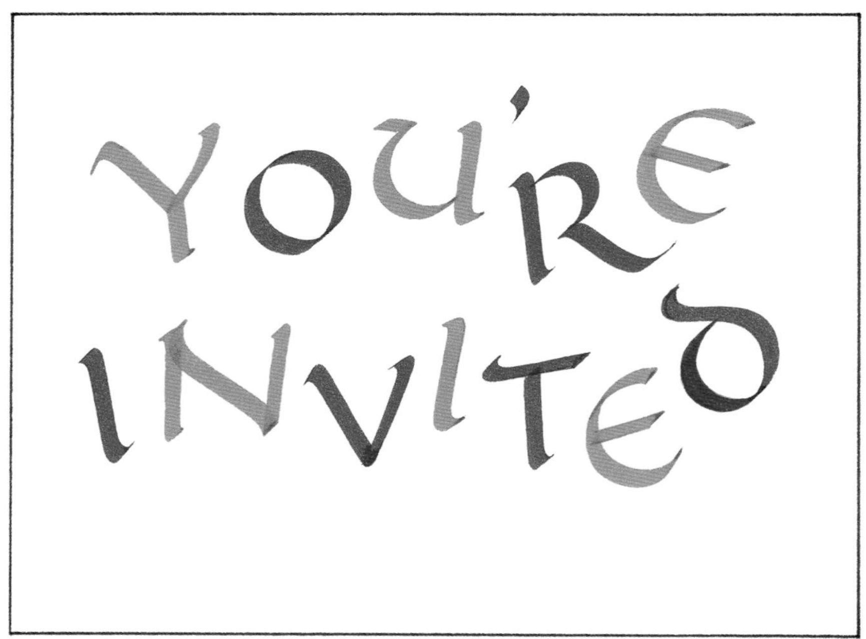

2

Calligraphy Vocabulary

These words are part of a basic calligrapher's vocabulary. You will hear (or read) these words when you study any style of calligraphy, in this book and in other calligraphy books. We will be using them again and again, so they will soon be familiar to you.

Now let's define the parts of the letters and the names of the lines you'll be using.

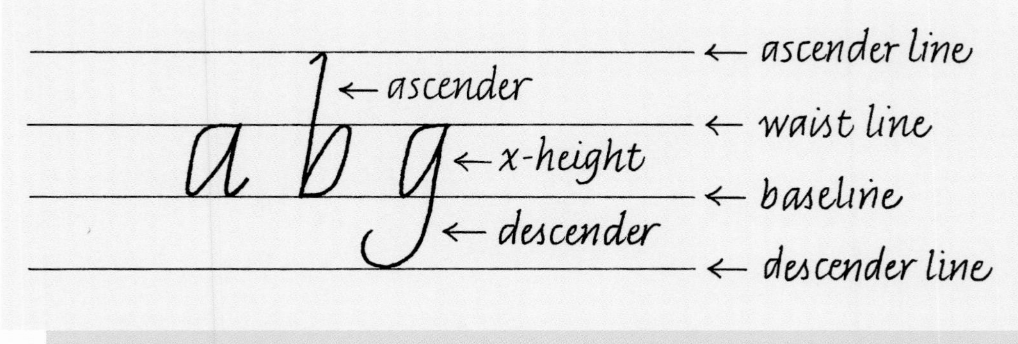

First, let's talk about the x-height. This will help you understand a few other terms.

x-height the height of the lowercase **"x"** and of all the small lowercase letters, such as the **a, c, e, m, n,** but not the **b** or the **h** or the **y.**

Here are some ways for describing the parts of letters.

ascender the upper part of the lowercase (minuscule) letters that extends above the x-height (for example, the top of the **b** and the **h**)

ascender line the guide line that marks the top of the minuscule letters with ascenders (For example, the top of the **b, h,** and **k** will touch the ascender line.)

baseline the line that most letters "sit" on (All lowercase except those with descenders rest on the baseline.)

descender the lower part of the minuscule letters that extends below the baseline (for example, the bottom of the **g, j,** and **y**)

descender line the guide line that marks the bottom of the minuscule letters with descenders

minuscule a lowercase letter (We'll use both terms, *minuscule* and *lowercase,* in this book.)

waistline the line that marks the top of the x-height space

Here are other calligraphic terms that you'll find in this book.

bookhand a style of calligraphy used for writing the text of a book (Before printing was invented, all books were written by hand.)

calligraphy beautiful writing

counter the "inside" of a letter

entrance stroke the small stroke that many letters begin with (sometimes called the "beginning stroke")

exit stroke the small stroke that many letters end with (also called the "ending stroke")

guard sheet a piece of paper used to protect the paper you are writing on. Your hand will rest on the guard sheet while you write.

guide lines the lines that you either draw on your paper or put under your paper to help you make your letters the correct size

hairline the thinnest stroke your pen can make

hand a style of calligraphy

majuscule a capital letter (In this book we will use the word **capital,** but it's good to know the word *majuscule* as well.)

nib the pen point (See Chapter 3, "Tools and Materials," for more about nibs.)

pen angle the relationship between the edge of the nib and the baseline (see Chapter 5, "Getting to Know Your Pen.")

spacing the space between letters in a word

stroke any mark or line made with your pen

3

Tools & Materials

The materials you need for calligraphy are fairly simple. Some are available in an art-supply store or stationery shop; others are a little more difficult to find. To help you get started, here are some tools and materials that you will need.

Chisel-Edge Calligraphy Markers These are felt-tip pens with a special calligraphy nib. Many shops sell these markers, so when they are used up, you should be able to replace them. They are available in many different colors.

Chisel-edge markers come in different sizes. The size refers to the width of the nib, or the tip, of the marker. (We'll explain more in Chapter 5, "Getting to Know Your Pen.") The size number—in millimeters—is printed on the side of the marker. We will be using markers labeled 3.5 mm (millimeters) and 2 mm. You can either get markers with two ends, such as the Zig Calligraphy Marker or the Staedtler Calligraphy Duo, which have 3.5 mm on one end and 2 mm on the other end, or find two individual (with only one writing end) markers, one labeled 3.5 mm and another labeled 2 mm. Some markers with one end are made by Itoya, Marvy, and Y&H.

(If you have any trouble finding a 3.5-mm marker, a 3-mm one will also give you good results.)

Don't forget to put the cap back on the marker when you aren't using it. This prevents it from drying out.

Broad-Edge Calligraphy Fountain Pen with Two Nibs Find a fountain pen with a wide nib (labeled B or B-4) and a medium nib (labeled either M or B-2). (You will be able to change nibs. Otherwise, you'll need to look for two pens, each with the desired nib.) We will mostly work with the wide nib. Sheaffer and Manuscript both offer good- quality calligraphy fountain pens.

Ink Cartridges These are very easy to attach to your fountain pen. Just follow the instructions in the package. When the cartridge is empty, you can remove it and replace it with a new one. Most stationery stores sell these cartridges. The inks usually come in a lot of colors. You'll want about five of these.

Guide Lines In the back of this book (pages 117 to 127), we have prepared special printed guide lines to help you make your letters the right size. Each page is marked with the calligraphy style and type of pen you will be using. You should be able to see these lines well when you place them under a sheet of white paper.

Although they cannot be easily removed from the book, make photocopies of these pages in a copy shop. Be sure that the book is held flat when the copies are made so that they look the same as the guide lines in the book. It's a good idea to make a copy of each of the guide lines before you begin to write so that they will be available when you want to use them.

These calligraphy fountain pens use ink cartridges. You can have fun using different colors of ink. Kneaded or plastic erasers come in handy for erasing pencil lines.

You will also need to get some other materials.

Paper You will need smooth white paper without lines. Your paper should be thin enough to see the guide lines that you place underneath it. If you buy it in an art-supply store, ask for "layout paper." Layout paper is thin, but not as thin as tracing paper (which isn't good for calligraphy).

Don't buy special "calligraphy paper." It is usually too expensive and sometimes not good for calligraphy!

Ordinary paper used in photocopiers (copy machines) is often very good for practicing calligraphy. You can test the paper by making a line with your fountain pen. If the paper absorbs the ink, it is not going to be good for calligraphy.

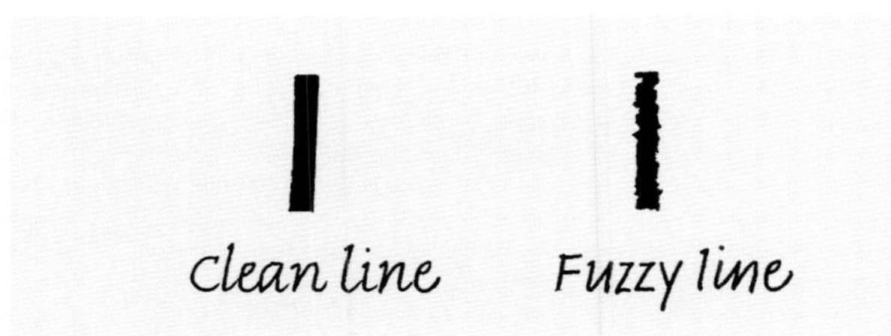

Pointed Markers Any kind of felt-tip marker is OK for learning the "skeleton forms" of letters, but a marker with a medium point may be easier to work with than a fine-point marker.

Pencil We will use a normal #2 pencil. You can try some exercises in this book using pencil and pointed marker to see which way is easier for you.

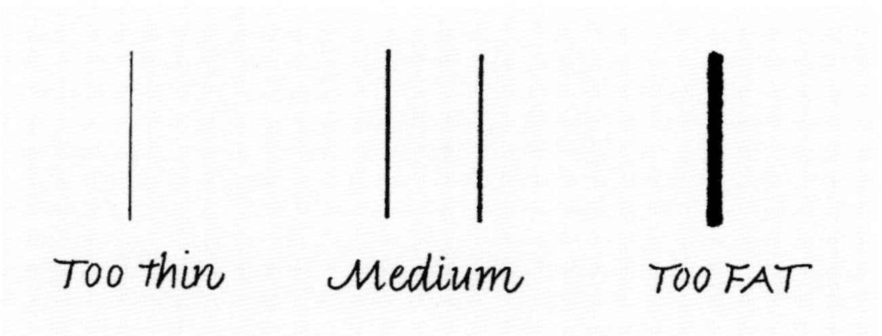

That's it! There are lots more art materials for calligraphers—dip pens, brushes, paints, papers, and all kinds of ink. But this is all you'll need to begin with.

And now, it's time to begin.

4

Getting Ready to Write

For your best calligraphy, sit this way...

Not like this...

And never like this...

Before you begin writing, here are a few things to think about. Don't skip this chapter! It will be much easier to learn calligraphy if you follow these simple directions.

HOW TO SIT

Sit up with your feet on the floor. You should be able to move your hand and arm easily and see what you are doing. If you are sitting on one foot, leaning sideways, or are off balance, your calligraphy will not be your best!

HOW TO HOLD THE PEN OR PENCIL

Hold your pen or pencil between your thumb and middle finger, resting it on your middle finger. Put your index finger lightly on top of the pen or pencil to help guide it. Your hand should look like this...

Here's the correct way to hold a pen.

Not like this...

...and never like this...

Don't hold your pen too tightly; your hand will get tired.

HOW TO HOLD YOUR PAPER

Tip your paper slightly uphill to the right if you are right-handed, and tip it downhill if you are left-handed.

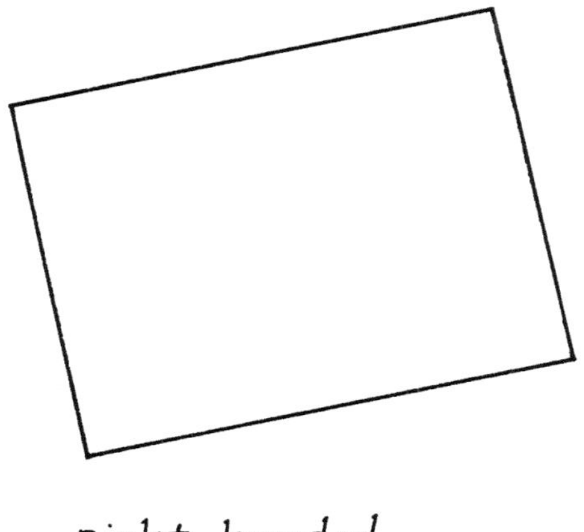

Right-handed position

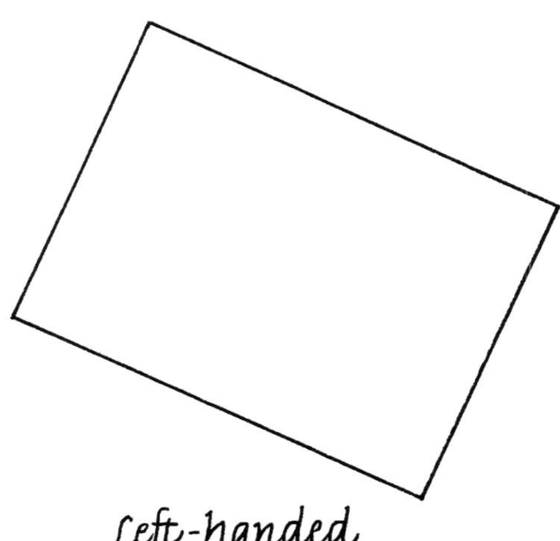

Left-handed position

GUARD SHEET

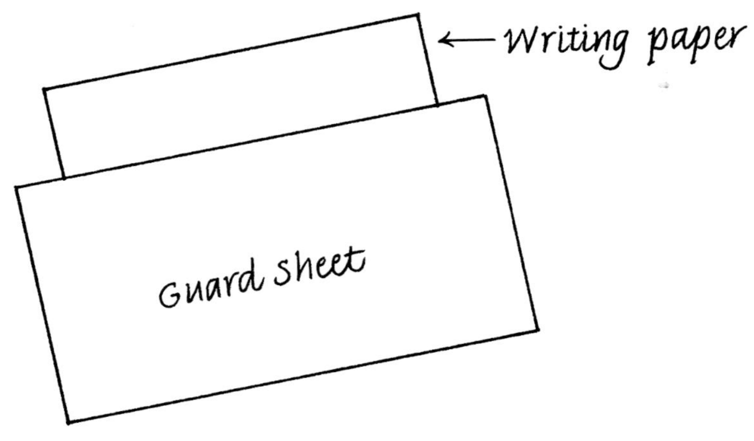

Place a clean sheet of paper over the page you are writing on, so that your hand has something to rest on. This is called the **guard sheet.** It will help keep the paper clean. It should be positioned just under the line you are writing on. As you continue to write, you can move the guard sheet down, so that your hand never touches the paper you are writing on.

LIGHT

You always need good light to see what you are doing. You can either work near a window or use a lamp. If you are right-handed, the light should be on your left side, and if you are left-handed, it should come from the right. That way, the shadow of your hand will not fall where you are writing.

PRACTICE, PRACTICE

It is easier to learn *anything* if you practice! That goes for football and tap dancing as well as cooking and calligraphy.

Each time you try an exercise or an alphabet, practice it before going further. How much should you practice? That depends on you. If you are patient and try to do each exercise several times, your calligraphy will get better and better. It is probably a good idea to spend a little more time on each exercise than you think you need!

Try to do each exercise a few times until it begins to look like the example in the book. Then go on to the next one. We'll give you some "How to Practice" suggestions throughout the book.

REMEMBER

The more you practice, the easier it will get.

5

Getting to Know Your Pen

Let's begin by looking at the pens we will be using. The two different pens—the felt-tip calligraphy marker and the fountain pen—both have the same shape of edge or nib. It's called a broad-edge, or a **broad-edged pen,** and it looks like this.

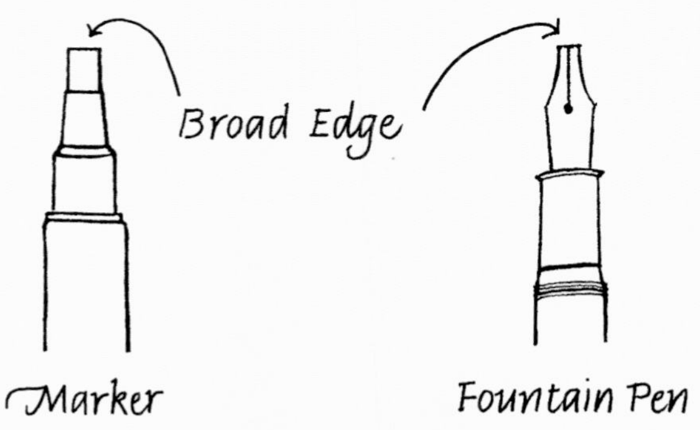

We're going to start with our **chisel-edge marker.** You can work with any color you like, or even change colors when you feel like it. But the most important thing is to **use the marker labeled 3.5 mm,** or if your marker has two ends, use the 3.5 mm end (not the 2 mm). Don't forget to put the cap back on the marker when you aren't using it.

To begin, remove the cap and hold the marker against your paper with the wide edge touching the paper. Move it to the right along its edge, without pressing too hard. You should get a thin line.

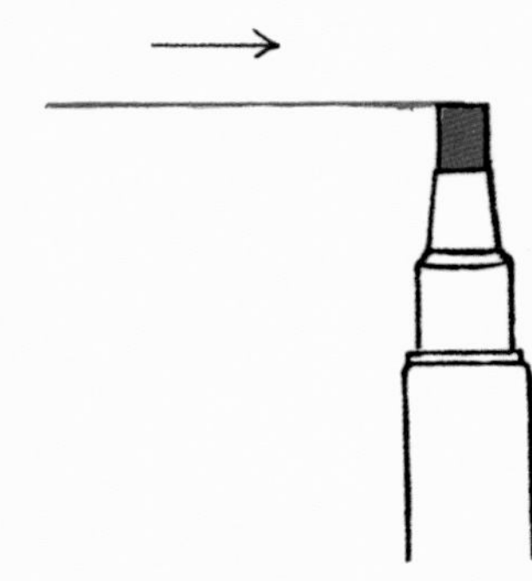

Now move it down the page; you should be seeing a thick line, like this.

Whenever you use this marker, or your fountain pen, the whole edge should touch the paper, not just a corner.

You will get a line that is thick, thin, or medium, depending on whether the pen or marker moves to the right, downward, or in any other direction.

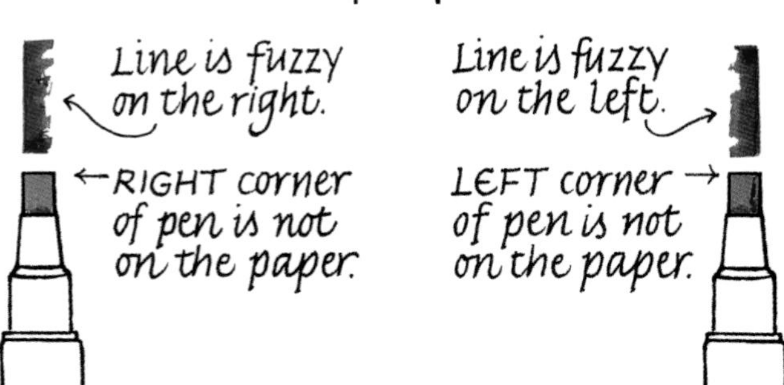

Line is fuzzy on the right.
RIGHT corner of pen is not on the paper.
Line is fuzzy on the left.
LEFT corner of pen is not on the paper.

REMEMBER
You never have to press hard on the marker! If you do that, you may spoil its edge.

GETTING READY TO WRITE

So that you'll have them on hand, make a photocopy of all guide lines found at the back of this book.

Now let's try some exercises. Take out the **guide lines** labeled **Pen Exercises,** and put it under a sheet of paper. Be sure you can see the lines through your paper. If you can't see the lines, you will either need to try some thinner paper or maybe use a stronger light. Tape or clip the sheet with guide lines into position under your paper so that it won't move around. Place another sheet of paper under your hand, partly covering the writing surface. This is your guard sheet, which we talked about in the previous chapter. Your setup should look like this

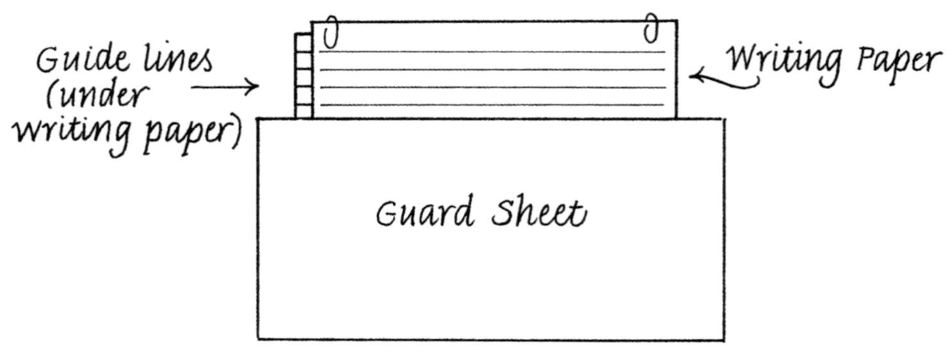

EXERCISE 1

The Zigzag

In order to do this exercise and to learn two of our four alphabets, you will need to hold the calligraphy marker so that the edge follows a diagonal line, like this.

Your guide lines are divided into squares or boxes. You are going to move the marker in a diagonal direction, first heading diagonally up and then diagonally down from left to right across the page.

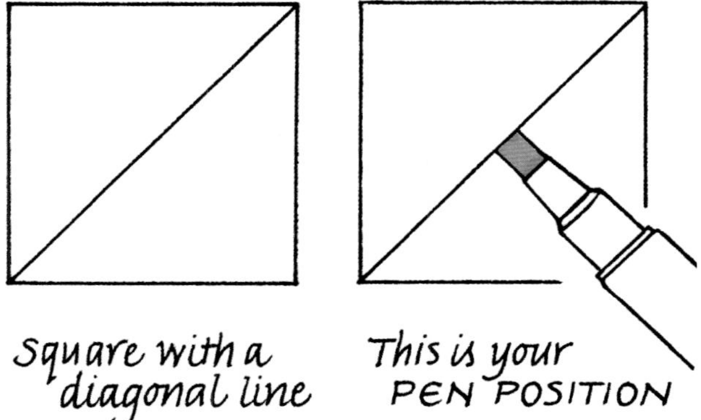

Square with a diagonal line
This is your PEN POSITION

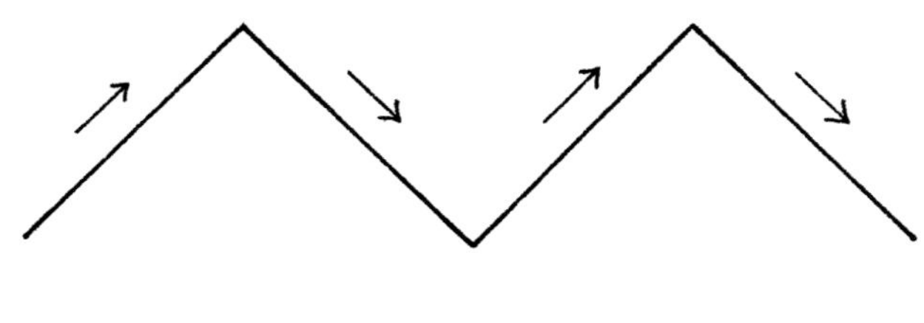

Upstrokes and Downstrokes The lines that go up are called **upstrokes** and the lines going down are called **downstrokes.** We will use the words *upstrokes* and *downstrokes* whether the lines are going straight up and down or diagonally up and down. When you make your upstroke, if you hold your pen in this diagonal position, as in the illustration at the top of the page, the lines you make will be thin. When you make the downstroke, you should get a thick line. But that only works when you keep the edge of your pen or marker in this position without turning it in your hand.

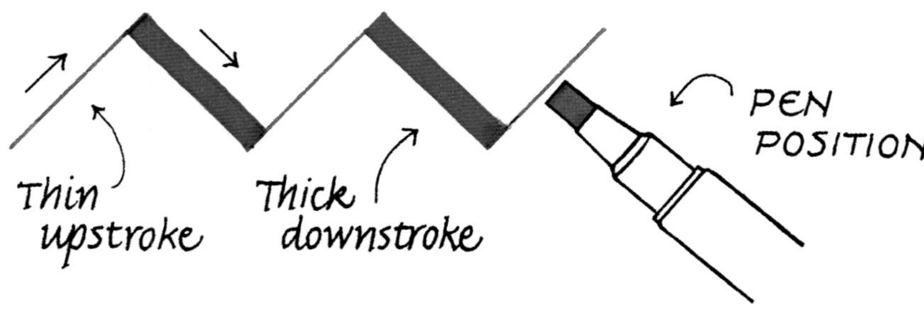

Try making a few lines of zigzags. Then try making some designs with zigzags. Here are a few possibilities, but you can try to invent some of your own.

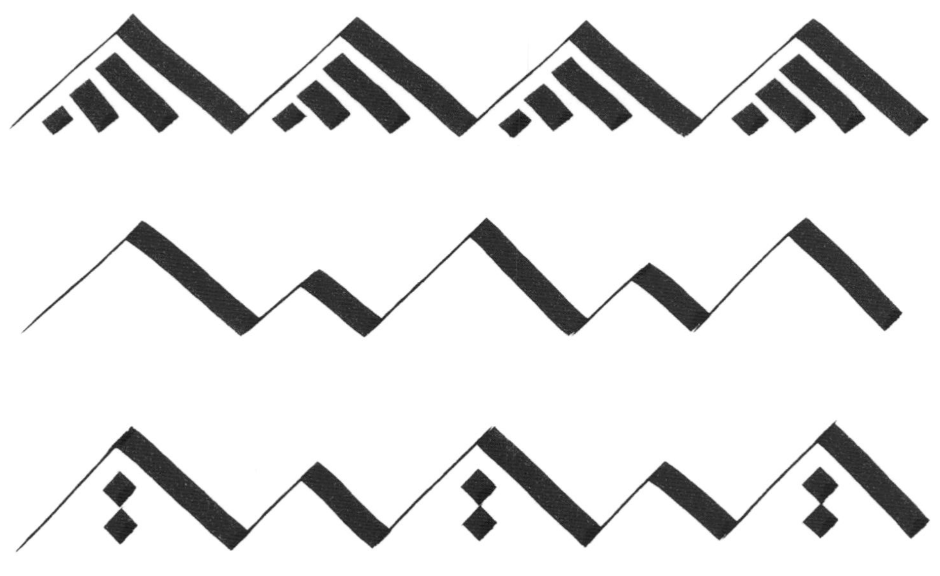

EXERCISE 2

Other Shapes

We are still holding the marker like this.

From now on we're going to call this the **diagonal pen position.** For those of you who have learned about angles in your math class, this is also called a **45° (45-degree) pen angle.** We'll use both terms in this book: diagonal pen position and 45° pen angle. Let's make some vertical and horizontal lines, holding our markers in the diagonal position.

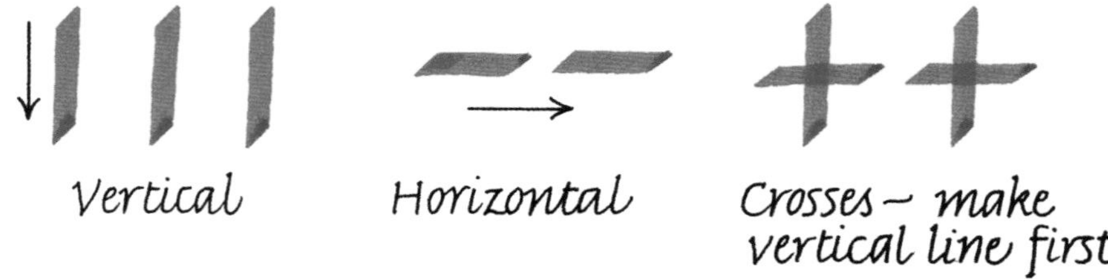

Now let's try some wavy lines and some curves.

Try some patterns or designs combining different parts of this exercise. Here's an example.

Make up some of your own designs, but always remember the rules of calligraphy.

We're going to learn two alphabets using the diagonal or 45° pen angle, and two using a different pen position. Let's start with the two 45° pen angle alphabets, Italic and Gothic. In Chapter 10, "A New Pen Position," we'll talk about the **flattened pen position,** which will be used for the other two alphabets.

1 Basic Rule of Calligraphy

When making letters in a particular alphabet, always hold the pen in the same pen position (or at the same pen angle).

PART II

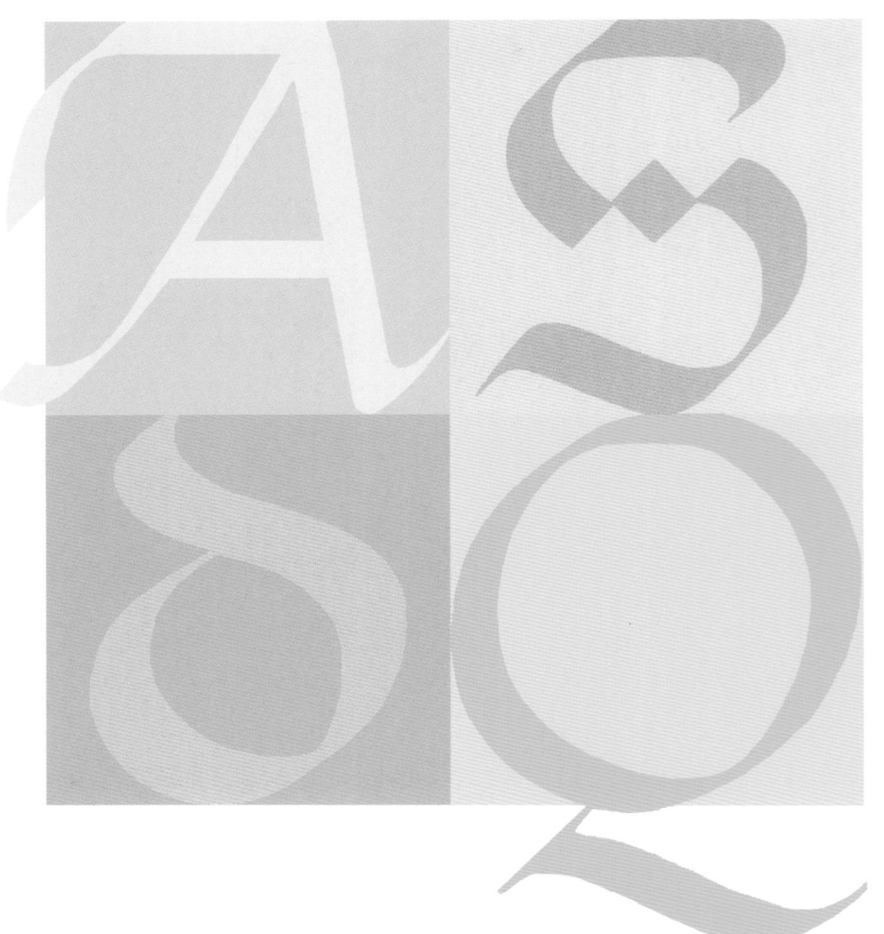

The Alphabets

6

Italic Calligraphy

Lowercase (Minuscule) Letters

This beautiful alphabet was originally a handwriting style used 500 years ago in Italy, during the Renaissance. It is easy to read and not so different from penmanship taught in schools today. Italic is written at a slant. The letters lean slightly forward.

like this

but not like this or this

We're going to start with the Italic lowercase letters, also called the **minuscules.** Take out the page of guide lines labeled **Italic #1** and place it under a sheet of paper. Don't forget to tape (easy-to-remove masking tape works nicely) or clip it into position so that it won't move around.

Let's start with an ordinary pencil or a pointed marker. If you are using a marker, don't use a really fine one or the lines will be too thin. First, let's look at the whole alphabet in its simplest—"skeleton"—form.

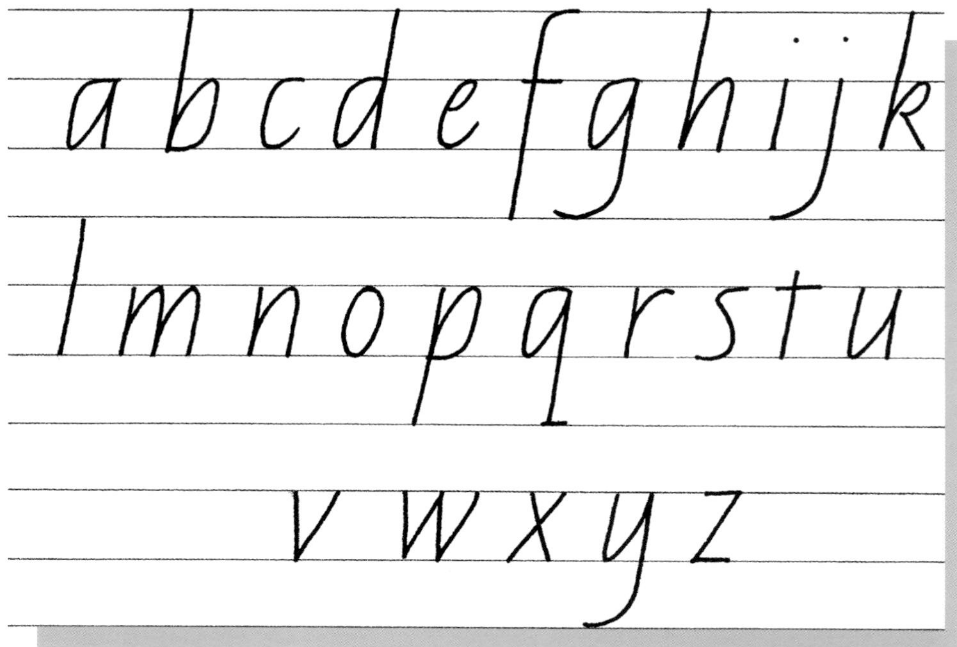

Notice that all the letter parts are the same size. The smaller letters, like the a, c, and e, fit into one space; and the longer ones with an upper part (ascender), like the b and the h, or a lower part (descender), like the g and the y, occupy two spaces. Only the f needs three full spaces.

2 Basic Rule of Calligraphy

Lowercase letters have three possible parts:
1. the main portion, known as the x-height
2. the upper part, called the ascender
3. the lower part, called the descender

Entrance and Exit Strokes Now let's add a little beginning and ending stroke to some of the letters. The beginning stroke is known as the **entrance stroke,** and the ending stroke is the **exit stroke**.

The letters are beginning to look more like calligraphy and less like "printing."

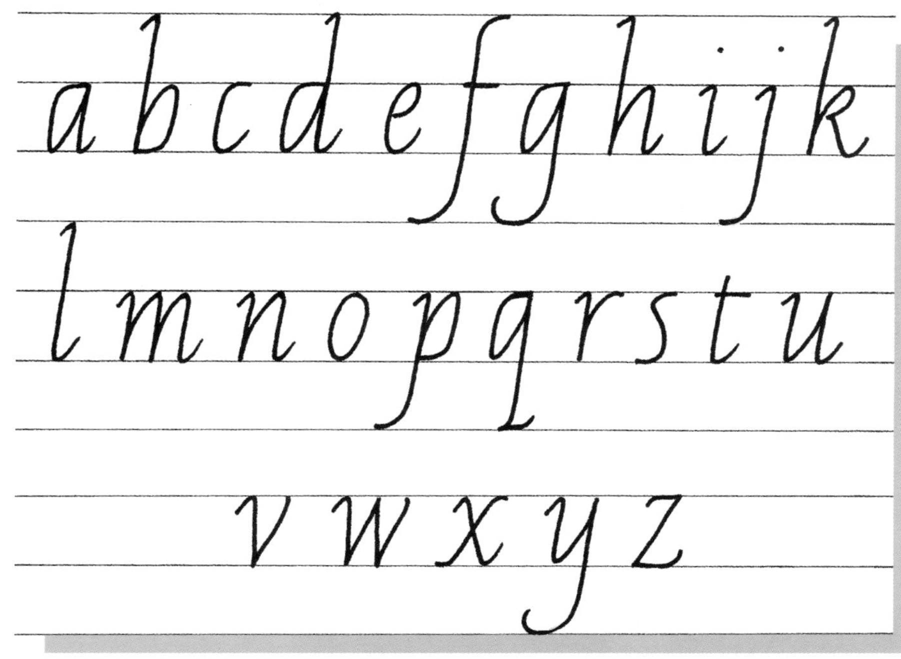

ITALIC LOWERCASE LETTER FAMILIES

We can divide these letters into families. Each family of letters has one repeated shape or line. Remember, we're just looking at lowercase, or minuscule letters.

The Straight-Line Family

Here are the **i, j, t, l,** and **f.**

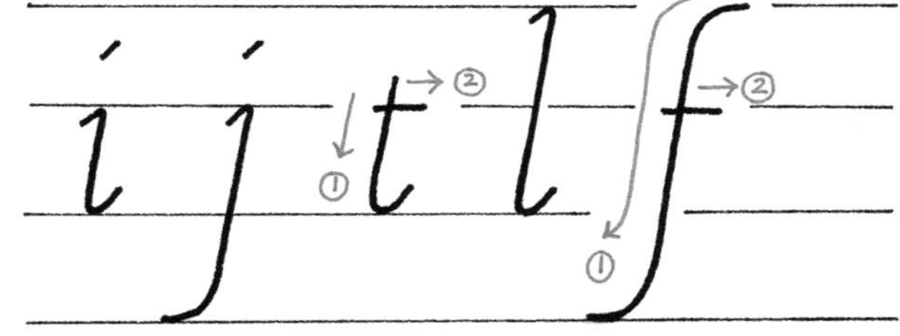

The a-Shape Family

This is the **a-shape.**

Start here

The top is flat

This side curves

This side slants

A little rounded

WRONG

Too straight

Too pointy

And here is the family, the **a, c, d, g, q, u,** and **y.**

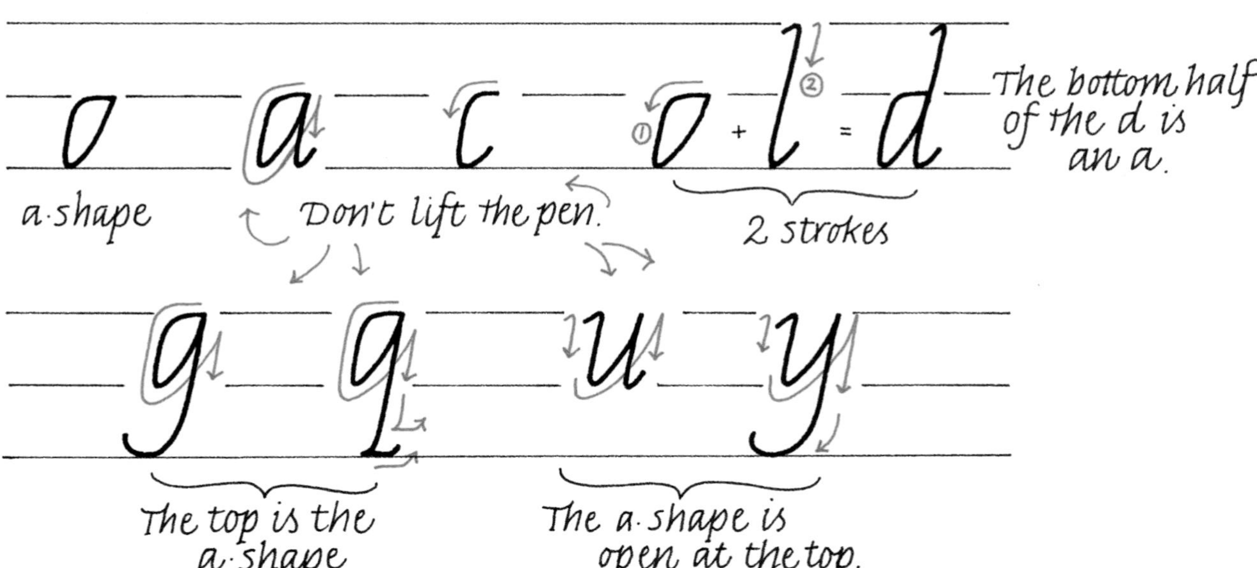
The bottom half of the d is an a.
a-shape
Don't lift the pen.
2 strokes
The top is the a-shape
The a-shape is open at the top.

All these letters are made without stopping—in one stroke—except the **d.** The **d** is an **a-shape** plus an **l.**

The b-Shape Family

This is the **b-shape.**

a little rounded
curve
slant
Start here
Flat

WRONG
Too pointy
Wrong direction
Too straight

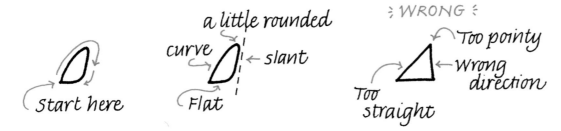

It is an upside-down a-shape. Here are the **b-shape** letters, the **b, h, m, n, r,** and **p.**

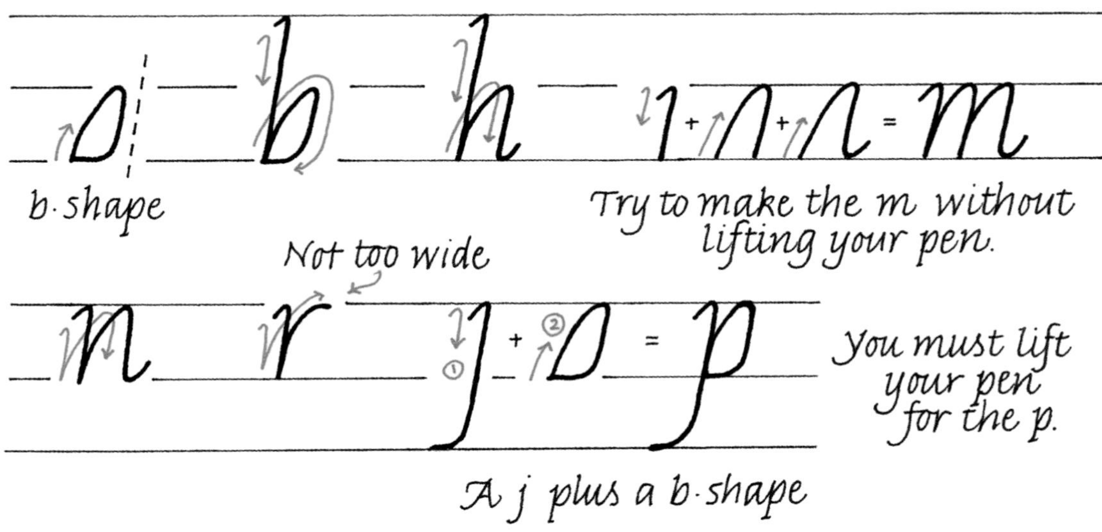

All these letters are made in one stroke (without taking the pen off the paper), except the **p.** The **k** is also part of this family, but it is more of a cousin than a sister or a brother.

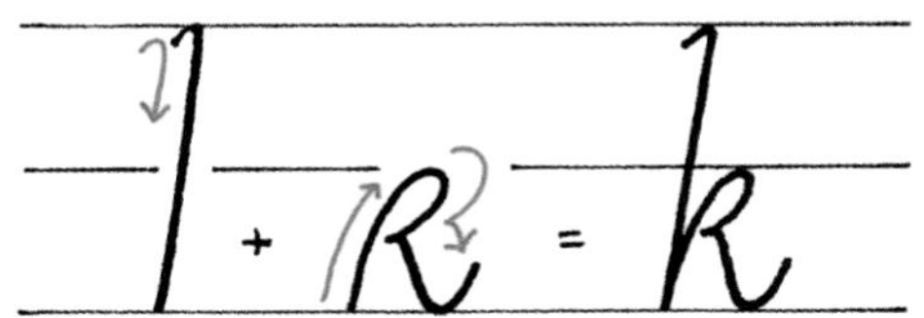

Try to make all the letters in the a and b families about the same width, with the exception of **m,** which is wider, and the **r,** which is a little narrower.

The Letters o and e

This is a very small family; it includes just the **o** and the **e.**

Start and end here
slant
2 strokes!

The Letters v and w

These two letters, the **v** and the **w,** are also closely related to each other. They are the only two letters that have points on the bottom. They are both shaped sort of like triangles.

The Others

Here's how you make the **s, x,** and **z.**

Try writing the letters in each family group using your pencil or pointed marker. Work slowly. If you write too quickly, they won't come out right. If you like, you can trace them a couple times before writing them on your own.

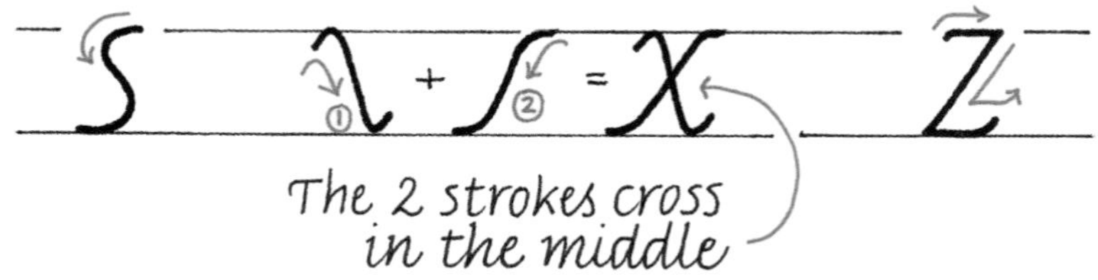
The 2 strokes cross
in the middle

We are now going to switch to the chisel-edge (calligraphy) marker, which will give you thick and thin lines. This is a wide marker, so you will be making large letters. You'll need to change guide lines to **Italic #2.**

We're going to use the word *pen* to refer to your calligraphy marker. Whatever you do with the marker you will do later with the fountain pen, but try these letters with the marker first, before switching to the fountain pen.

DIAGONAL PEN POSITION

Before we make any letters, let's review the pen position.

This is the **diagonal pen position,** or the 45° pen angle. Be sure you are holding your pen so that the edge follows the diagonal line in the picture. If you didn't do the zigzag exercises in Chapter 5, do them now!

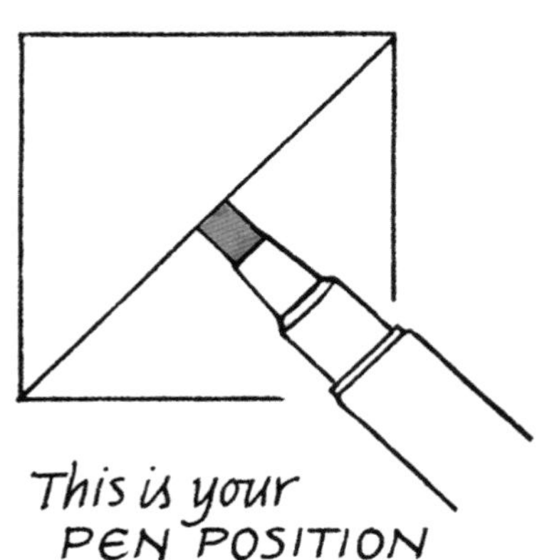

Try to remember to hold your pen in this position for all your Italic strokes, shapes, and letters. Your pen and your strokes will look like this.

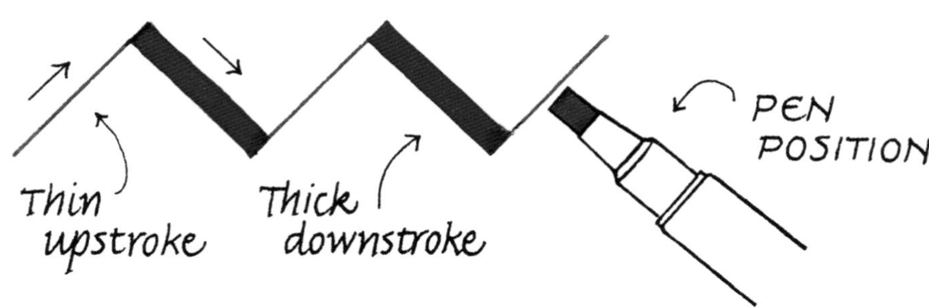

If your pen looks like this:

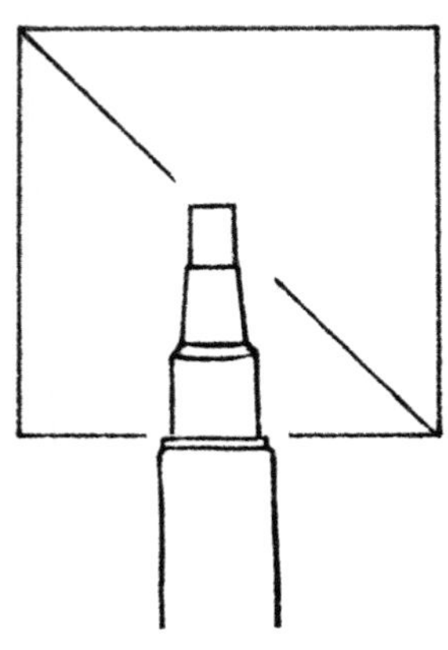

or like this:

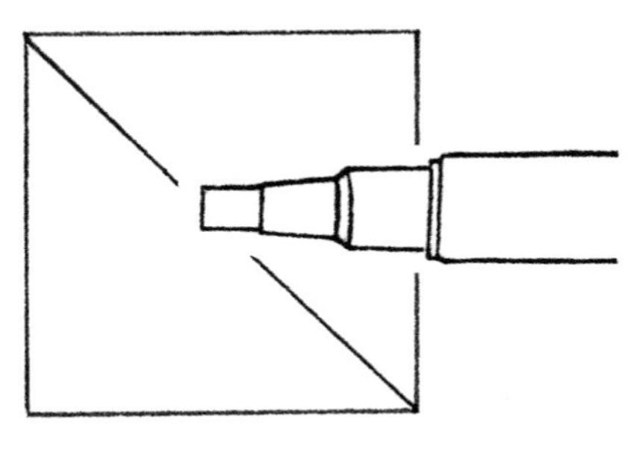

...You are holding it wrong. Keep practicing the correct pen position, and it will soon be easy.

Now, let's try making the Italic lowercase letters using your chisel-edge marker. They should look like this.

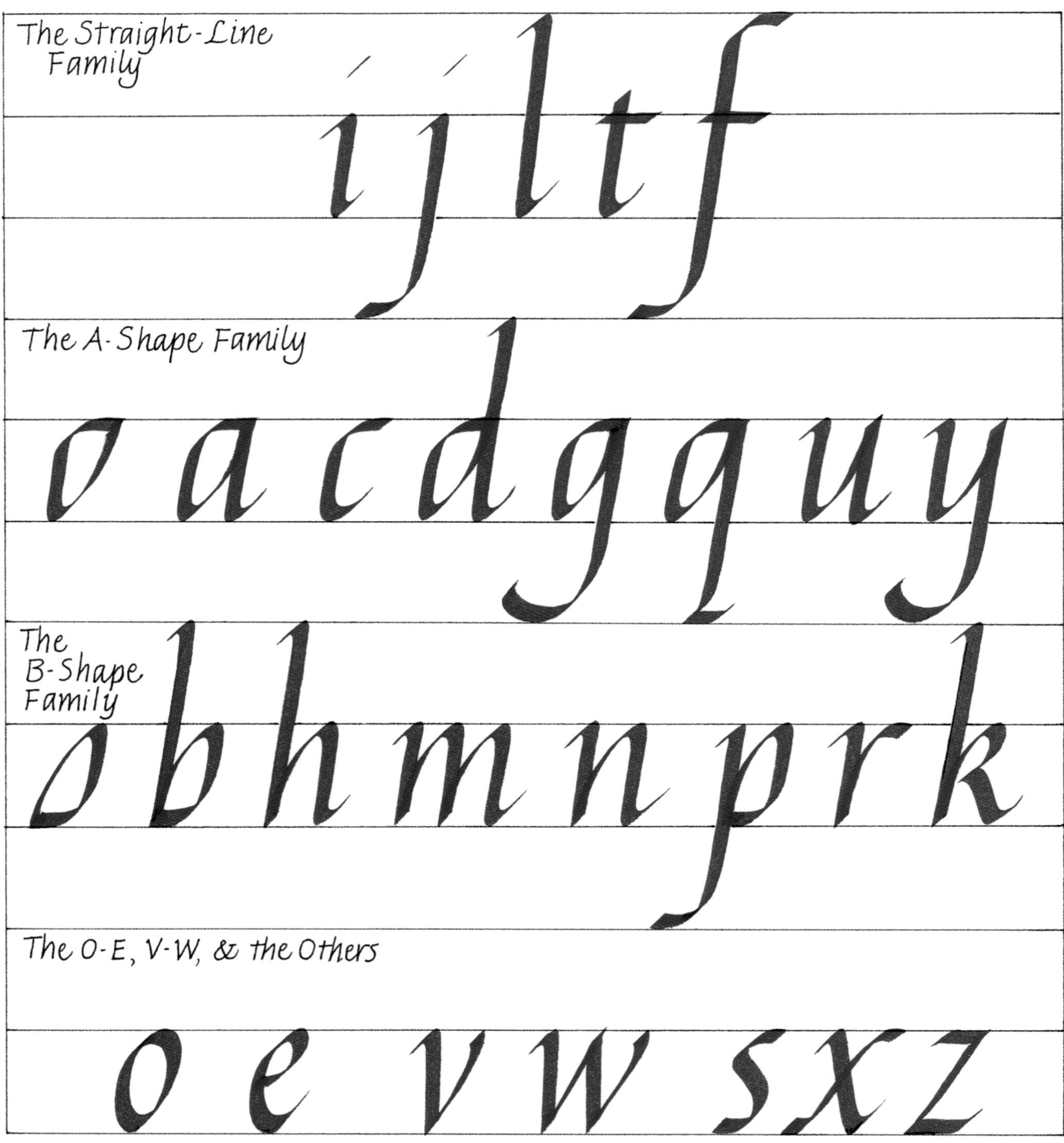

You can try tracing these letters a few times. This will help you get to know the shape and width of the letters.

Here are some mistakes that you can correct.

These letters are too WIDE:

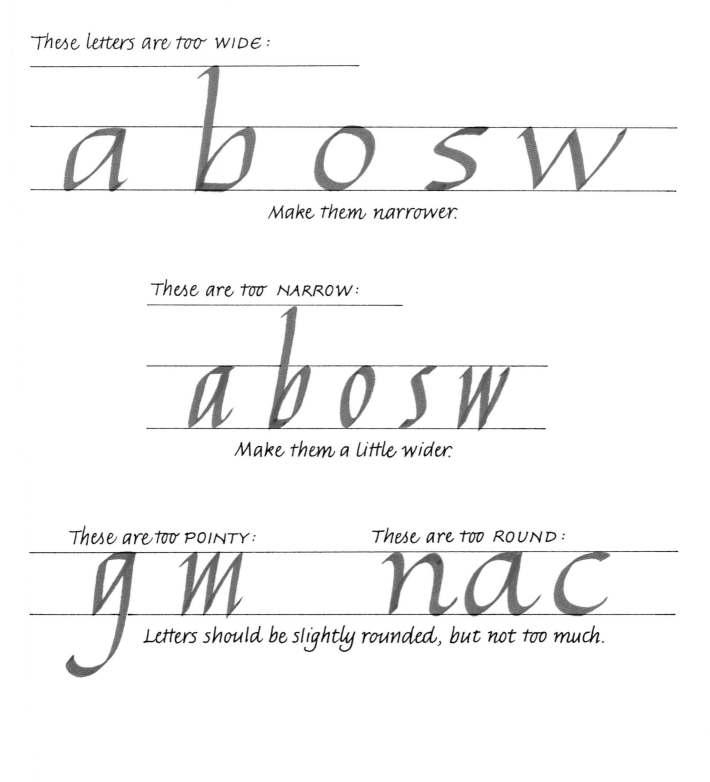

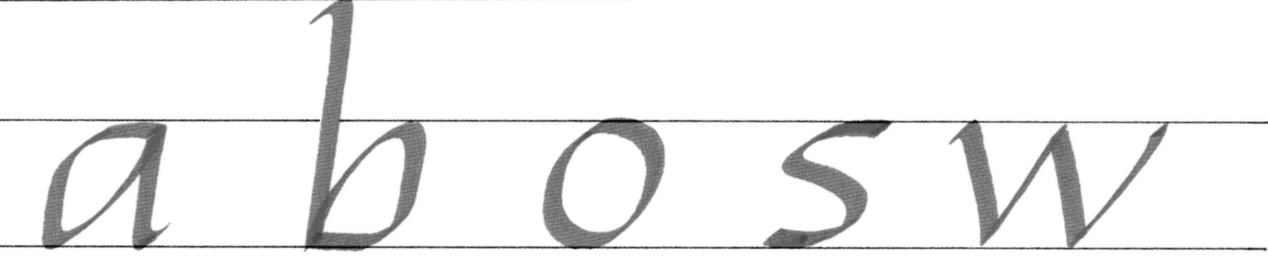

Make them narrower.

These are too NARROW:

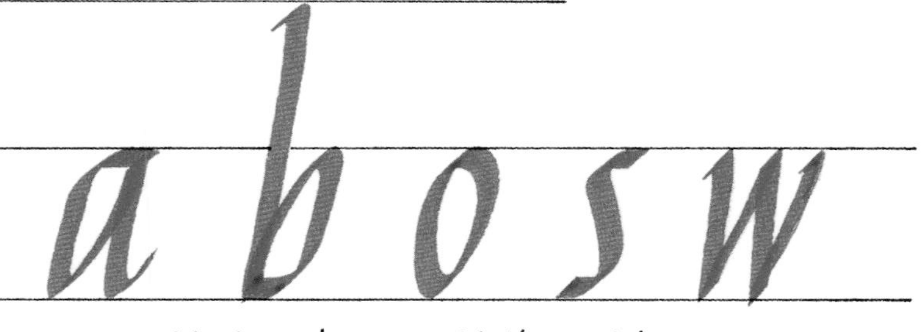

Make them a little wider.

These are too POINTY:

g m

These are too ROUND:

n a c

Letters should be slightly rounded, but not too much.

TOO TALL:

bna

TOO SHORT:

upe

Be sure to use your guidelines!

These letters are SLANTING too much or in too many different directions:

mql abn

your Italic guidelines have SLANT LINES to help you make your letters slant correctly.

SPACING

In order to make words in calligraphy, we have to learn something about **spacing.** Spacing refers to the space inside the letters and also the space between letters. Remember the third basic rule of calligraphy.

3 Basic Rule of Calligraphy

When making words, the space between letters appears to be about the same as the space inside the letters.

Let's see what that looks like.

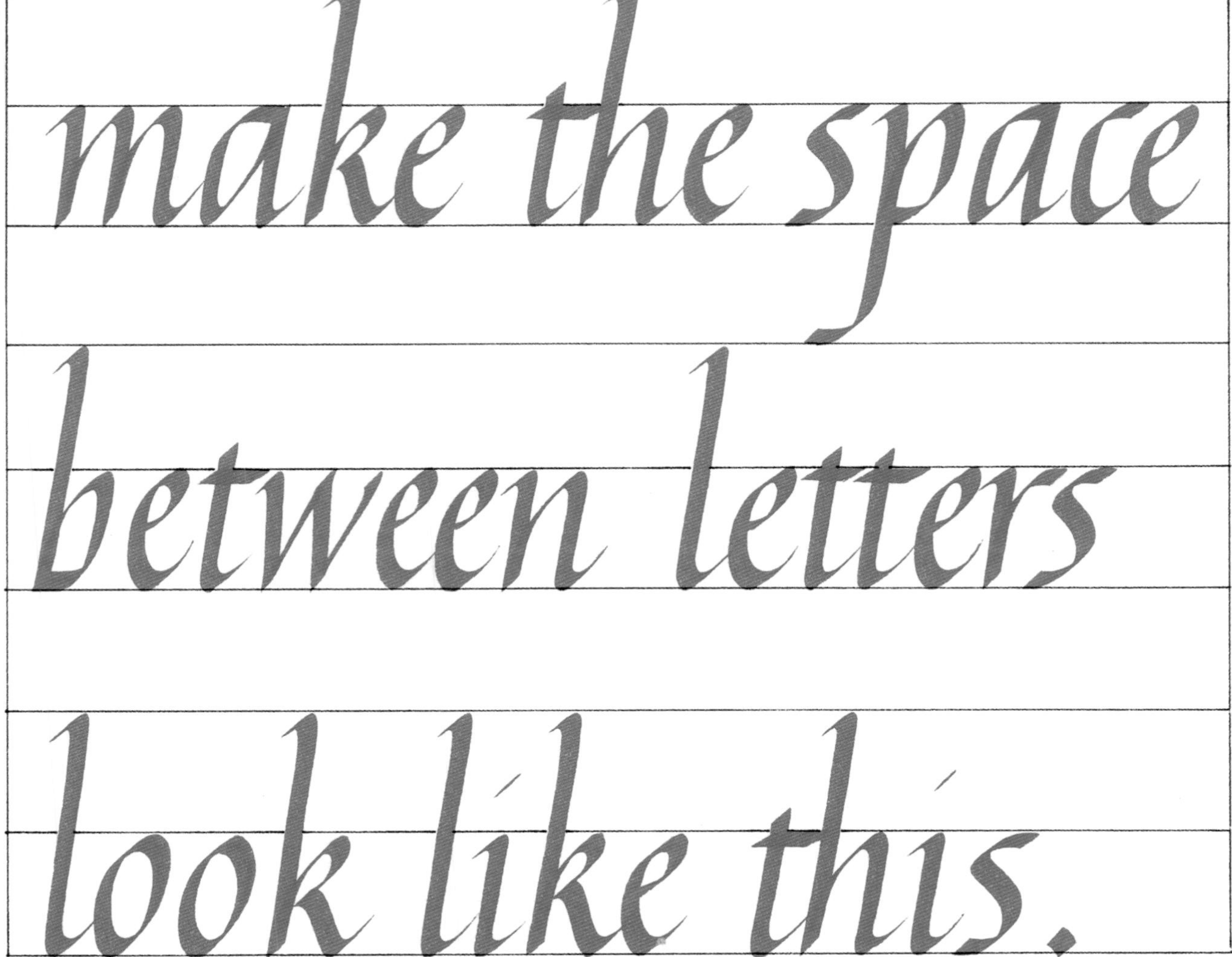

make the space
between letters
look like this.

Remember that most of the letters—all the **a-shape** and **b-shape** letters—are approximately the same width. When the letters are odd-shaped, like the **k,** the **s,** or the **x,** we try to make the white space around them look equal to the space inside the **a** or the **b,** like this.

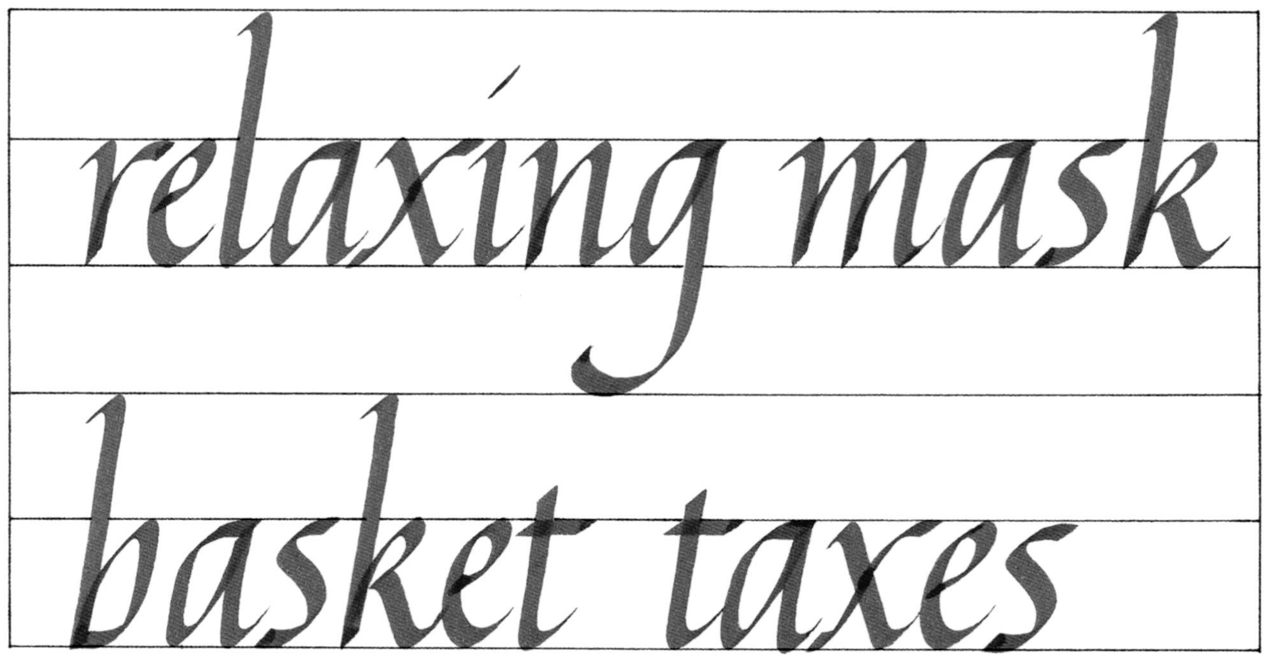

NOW TRY YOUR FOUNTAIN PEN

It's time to try the Italic minuscules with your fountain pen, using the wider (B or B-4) nib. The nib of the fountain pen is narrower than the edge of the calligraphy marker. It will therefore make strokes that are narrower than the strokes you make with the marker. Here's one more rule.

4 Basic Rule of Calligraphy

When you use a wide nib, the letters will be taller and heavier than the letters you make with a narrower nib.

This is another way of saying that **the height of the letters is proportional to the width of the nib.** Chances are, you haven't studied proportions yet in school. But if you look at the example below, this rule should become clear.

The letters you make with your fountain pen, which is narrower than the calligraphy marker, need to be shorter than the ones you just made with the marker. So we will now use the guide lines labeled **Italic #1.** These lines will be used for both the pointed marker (or pencil) letters and the fountain pen.

Put these guide lines under a sheet of white paper and try to write the letters a few times with your fountain pen. Concentrate on family relationships and the shapes and widths of the letters. Then try writing some words.

When you have done that, you will be ready to try writing some lines of text. Choose a poem or some song lyrics that you especially like. Write it all lowercase until you have learned the Italic capital letters in the next chapter.

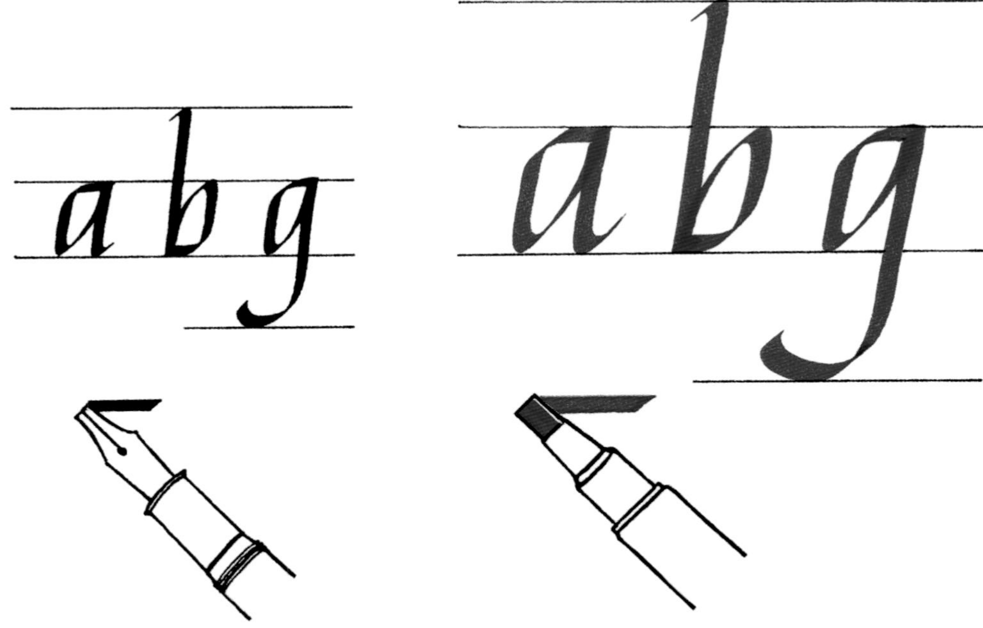

7

Italic Calligraphy

Capital Letters

Italic capital letters can be simple or decorative. We're going to learn the more decorative capitals. The simple capitals are slanted versions of the Roman capital letters that you will see in Chapter 13.

Here are some basic facts.

1. The Italic capitals are taller than the lowercase **a** and shorter than the **b.** Or, to put it another way, they are about halfway between the x-height (height of all the short lowercase letters) and the ascender (height of the **b, h, k, l**). Here is what this looks like.

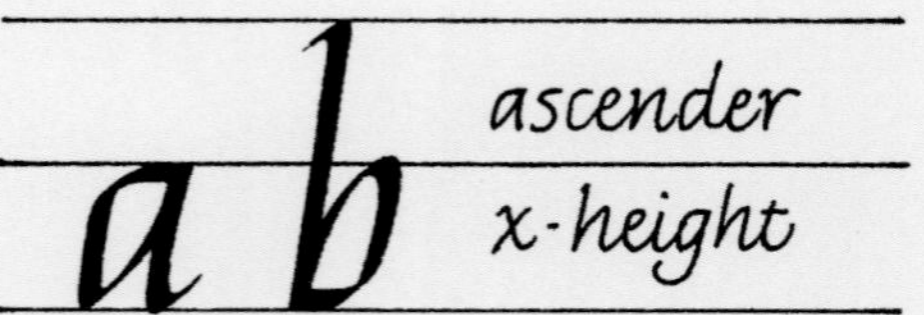

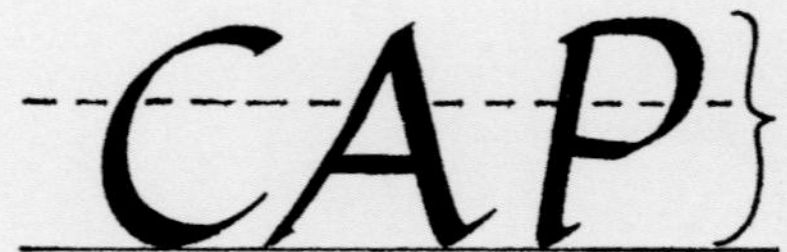

2. The decorative capitals are called **swash capitals.** We use the word swash to describe the flourish on the upper left side of many of these letters, such as the **M.**

3. The capitals are slanted, just like the lowercase.

We're going to learn these letters by starting with their skeleton forms, using pencils or pointed markers. After that we'll use the chisel-edge calligraphy markers, just as we did with the Italic minuscules.

First let's look at the skeleton forms and compare them in height with the lowercase letters.

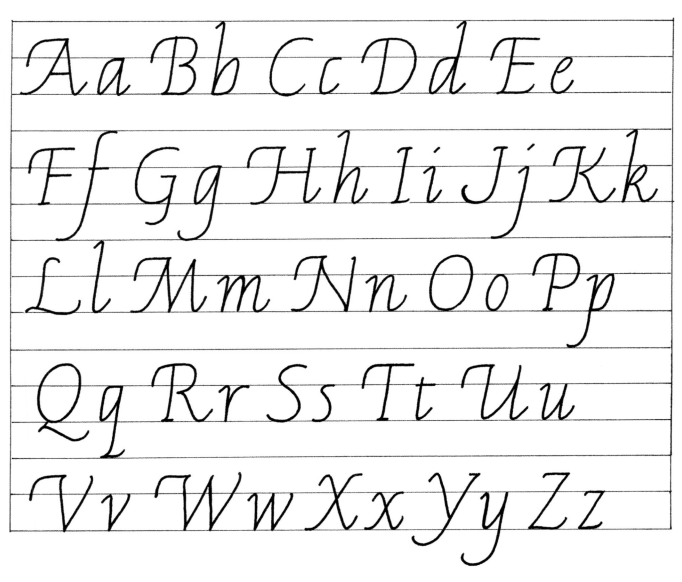

Aa Bb Cc Dd Ee
Ff Gg Hh Ii Jj Kk
Ll Mm Nn Oo Pp
Qq Rr Ss Tt Uu
Vv Ww Xx Yy Zz

Now we're going to try writing them in pencil or pointed marker. We'll start with some basic strokes and then divide them into groups. Use the same guide lines you started with in the previous chapter, labeled **Italic #1.**

THE DOWNSTROKE

Here's the **basic downstroke.**

Small curve

Too curvy

WRONG

This will be the first stroke of the **B, D, E, F, P, R,** and **T.** Notice that it slants a little, exactly the same amount as your lowercase letters.

It's the same as the descender of the **q.**

Letter Slant

This is the first stroke of all the letters in this group. The little stroke on the bottom (the "foot" of the letter) is sometimes quite small, sometimes medium size, and sometimes long, depending on which letter you are making. Try it three ways.

Notice it ends by going up a little at the right.

Short foot Medium Long

MORE STROKES

Now let's add a second stroke to form this first group of capitals. Remember that the basic downstroke is always made first. The **T**, **F**, **P**, and **R** all have the short stroke on the bottom.

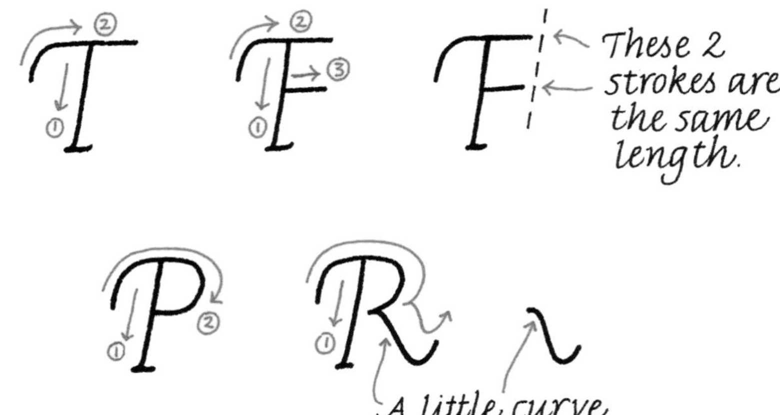

These 2 strokes are the same length.
A little curve

Here are some mistakes.

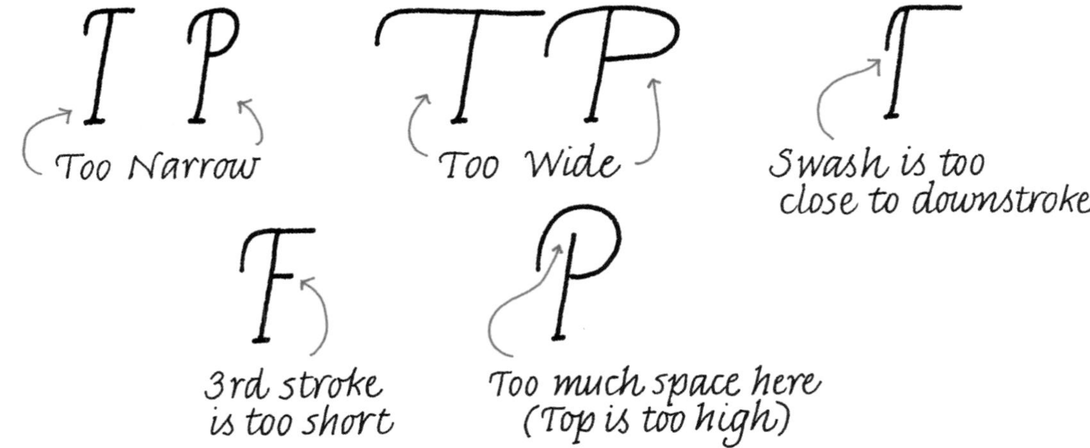

Swash is too close to downstroke
3rd stroke is too short
Too much space here (Top is too high)

The **B** has a medium-size foot.

The strokes meet here

These are common mistakes when making the **B**.

Top heavy

Bottom heavy

The **E** and the **D** have the longest "foot." The top of the **E** is the same as the top of the **F** on page 39.

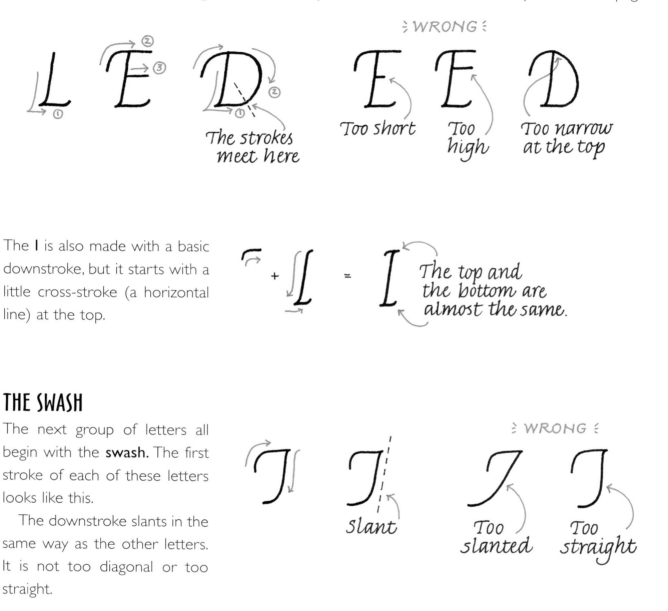

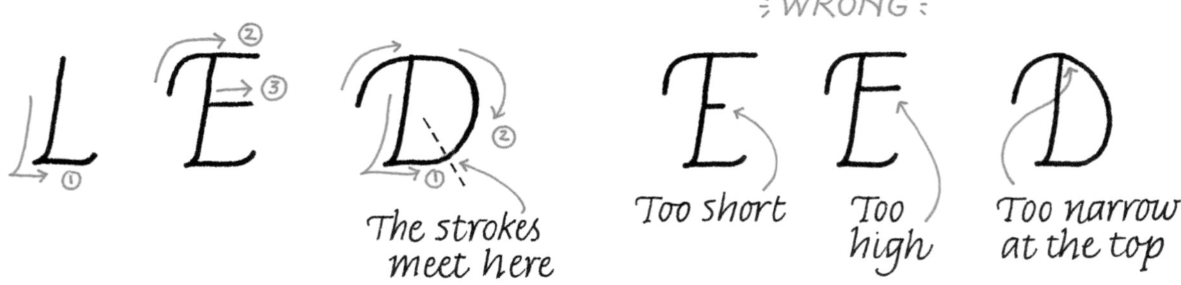

The **I** is also made with a basic downstroke, but it starts with a little cross-stroke (a horizontal line) at the top.

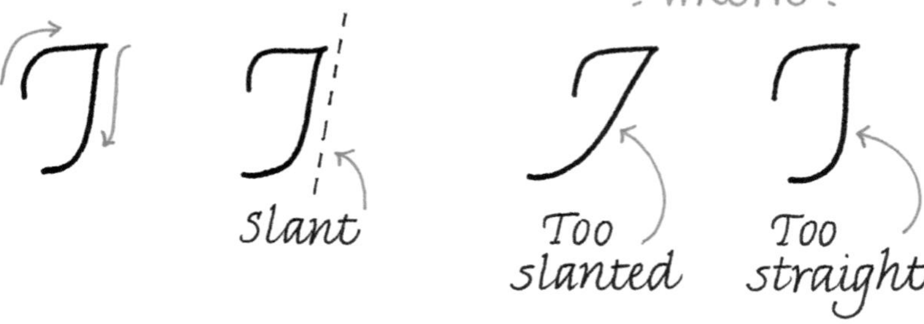

The top and the bottom are almost the same.

THE SWASH

The next group of letters all begin with the **swash.** The first stroke of each of these letters looks like this.

The downstroke slants in the same way as the other letters. It is not too diagonal or too straight.

WRONG

Slant

Too slanted

Too straight

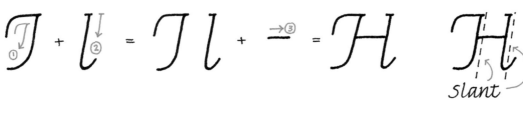

Let's try the **H, K, N,** and **U.**

The little cross-stroke on the top of the right side of the **H** is the same as the one on the top of the **I.** The **U** is a little different because the bottom of the first stroke goes to the right; in the other three letters it goes to the left.

Slant

Same as the R

A little curve

Almost the same as the lower-case u

The **A, M, V,** and **W** also start with the swash. On the **A** and the **M,** this stroke slants to the left more than it does on the **H.**

Slant

First stroke of A

First stroke of H

The **V** and the **W** both start with a stroke that is straighter (more vertical) than the **H.**

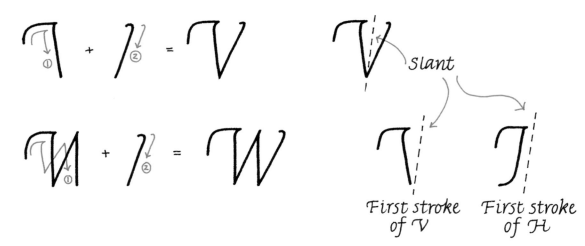

Slant

First stroke of V

First stroke of H

THE ROUND LETTERS

You have now done all the letters with a **swash**—15 out of 26. Now we'll try the "**round**" letters. The word round is in quotes because the "round" letters aren't circular, but they are rounder than the lowercase letters. These are the **O, C, G,** and **Q.** They all start with this stroke.

Make this curved stroke a few times. Now add the other strokes.

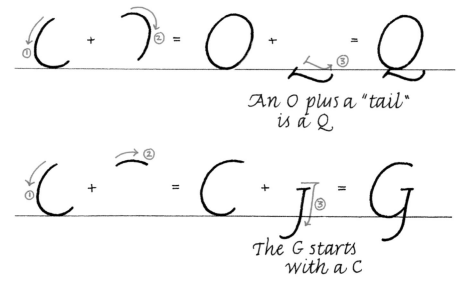

An O plus a "tail" is a Q

The G starts with a C

An **O** plus a tail will give you a **Q.** A **C** with a different tail becomes a **G.** This group—the **O-shape** letters—needs a little extra practice, so that they aren't...too wide, too narrow, squashed, or pointy.

Too wide
Too narrow
Squashed
Pointy

MORE CAPITAL LETTERS

And here are the other capital letters.

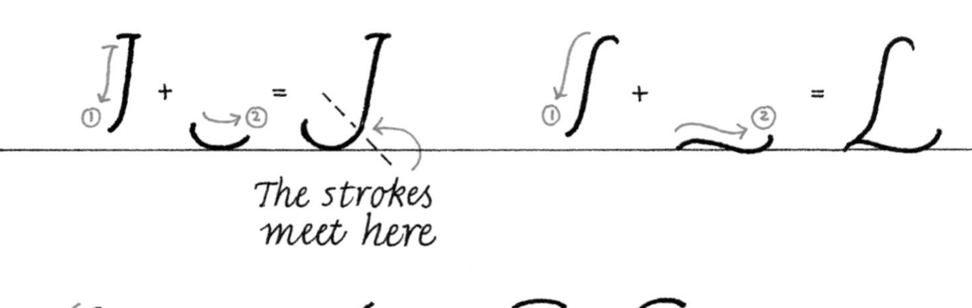
The strokes meet here

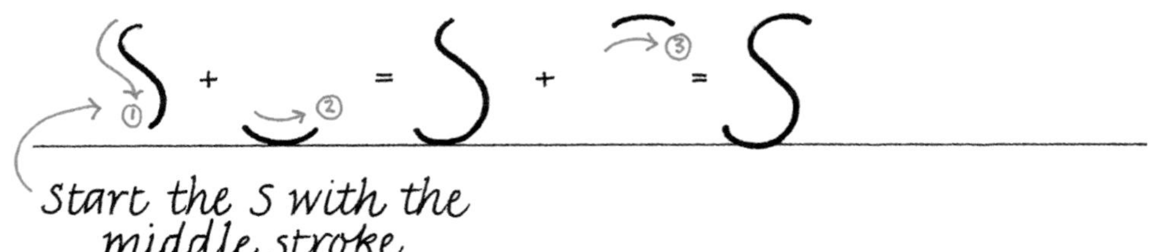
Start the S with the middle stroke

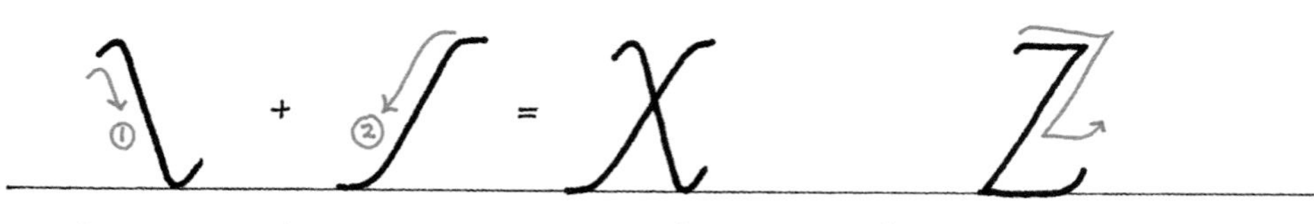
Same as the lower-case (only bigger)

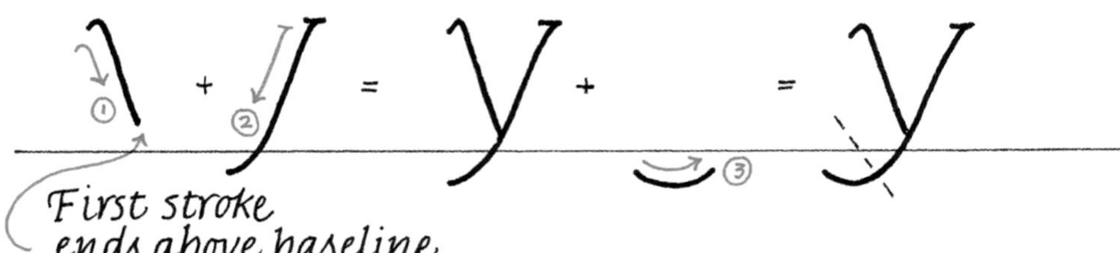
First stroke ends above baseline

Important! Remember that the capitals are parallel to the lowercase, even though they are mostly not made of straight lines. Letters like the **S**, the **X**, and the **Z** need special attention to make them slant properly.

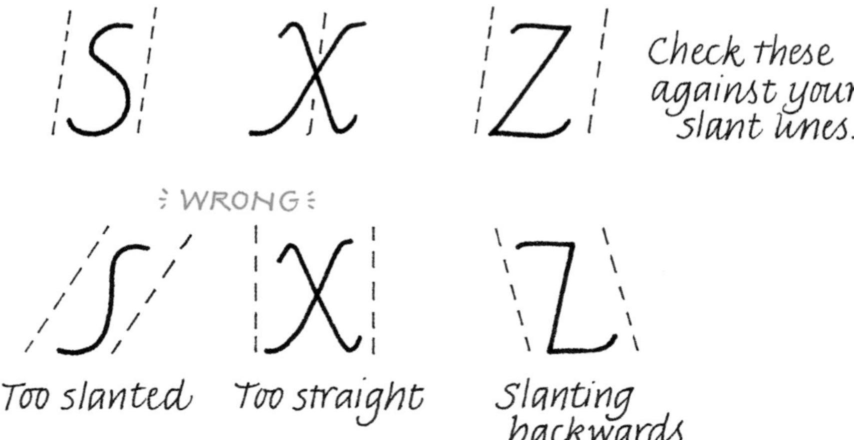

Check these against your slant lines.

Slanting backwards

USING YOUR CALLIGRAPHY MARKER

Now let's try the same letters with our calligraphy markers. Change to the other Italic guide lines (**Italic #2**) so that the spaces are big enough for this larger nib. See what the capitals should look like on page 45.

When you practice these letters, remember that your pen must be in the **diagonal pen position**, or the **45° pen angle**.

After you try these letters, write some names starting with a capital letter, using the calligraphy marker. Try to think about **spacing** (the space between the letters in the words), as well as the shape of the letters!

USING YOUR FOUNTAIN PEN

It's time to try the capitals with your fountain pen. Remember that the fountain pen has a narrower nib than the calligraphy marker, so you will need to change guide lines (again!). Use **Italic #1**, the same lines you used to practice the lowercase letters with your fountain pen.

It's a good idea to practice the capitals a few times with your fountain pen until they start to feel natural and look right. Then try writing a short text in Italic, starting each line with a capital letter.

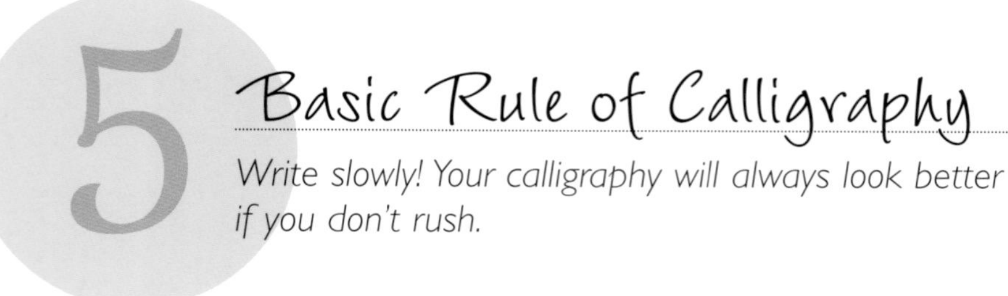

5
Basic Rule of Calligraphy
Write slowly! Your calligraphy will always look better if you don't rush.

I L L T F P R

B D E I

J H K N U

A M V W

C O C Q G

J L S X Y Z

Allison Bob

Christopher

Daniel Emily

Felix George

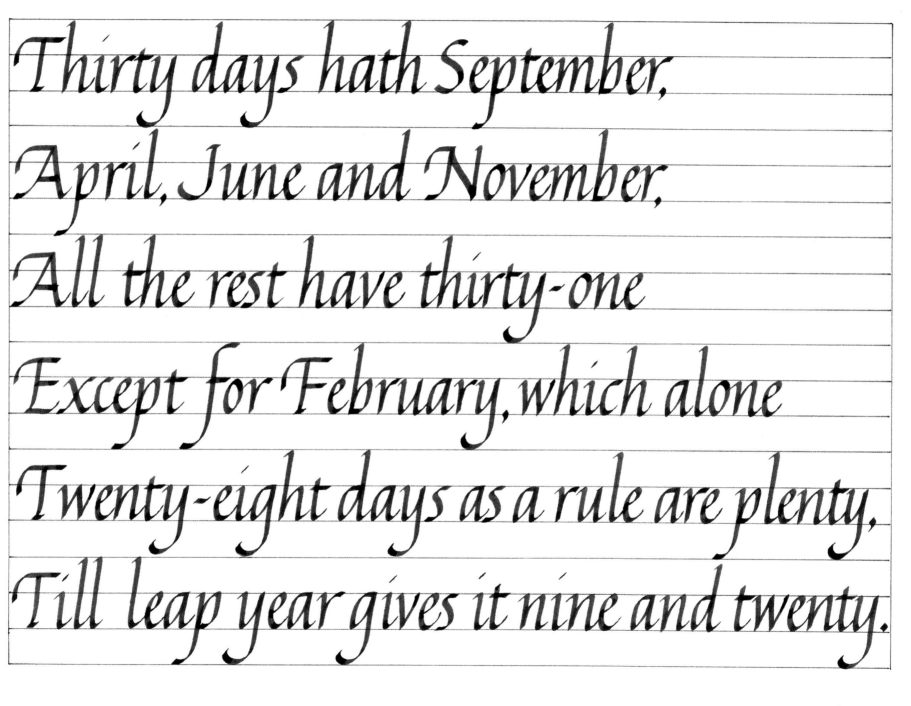

Thirty days hath September,
April, June and November,
All the rest have thirty-one
Except for February, which alone
Twenty-eight days as a rule are plenty,
Till leap year gives it nine and twenty.

8

Gothic Calligraphy

Lowercase (Minuscule) Letters

Everyone loves to learn Gothic calligraphy. It is very decorative and looks much harder to do than it is. It makes us think of "Merry Christmas" and "Season's Greetings" and "Diploma" and "Award," but it can be used for lots of other projects.

Gothic calligraphy is also called **Black Letter** because, in the 12th to 15th centuries (the Middle Ages) when it was used, there wasn't much money to make books. The scribes who did the writing (all books were written by hand in those days!) had to make the letters and the lines of writing very close together in order to squeeze as much as possible onto every page. Sometimes they also wrote very small. When we look at those books today, we cannot believe that anyone could do such beautiful calligraphy with such tiny letters! The result of all those black strokes squeezed tightly together was that the page looked very black, which is why we call Gothic calligraphy "Black Letter."

nemochte ane schaden. Do
untwanden en de boden des
soldanes. De keiser vor
do vort to komn de heyde
nen striden mit eme. vn̄
worden seghelos bi der st
at ere wart ane mate uele
gheslagen. Sin sone de
hertoghe wederic. wan de
wile de stat vn̄ herberge
de dar inne. En borch lach
binnen der stat. dar was
uppe de soldan. vor der bor

There are many different kinds of Gothic calligraphy, but we're going to learn just one style. This style, or "hand," is called **Textura,** and it was used in the 12th through the 14th centuries. When we use the word *Gothic* in this book, we really mean "Textura Gothic."

Unlike Italic, which has lots of thin lines, most strokes in Gothic calligraphy are thick. We are therefore going to skip the pencil/pointed marker part of our lessons and go directly to the calligraphy marker. If you try to write Gothic with a pencil, you'll see that it is almost impossible to do.

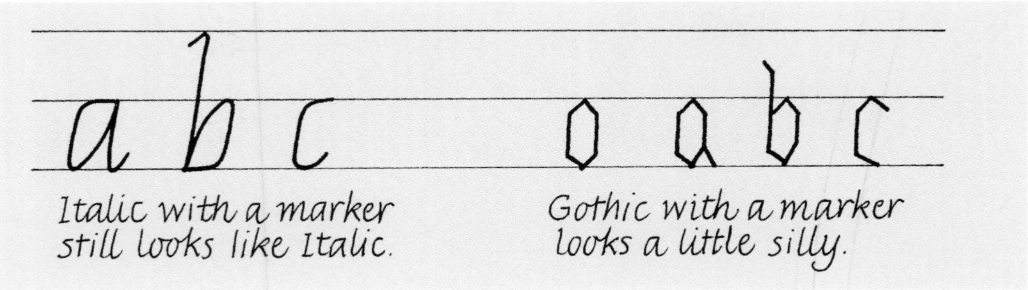

a b c
o a b c
Italic with a marker still looks like Italic.
Gothic with a marker looks a little silly.

So, here we go. Take out your **Gothic #1** guide lines and your calligraphy marker. Put the guide lines in position under a sheet of paper and warm up with a few zigzags, because Gothic is written with the same pen position as Italic (diagonal pen position).

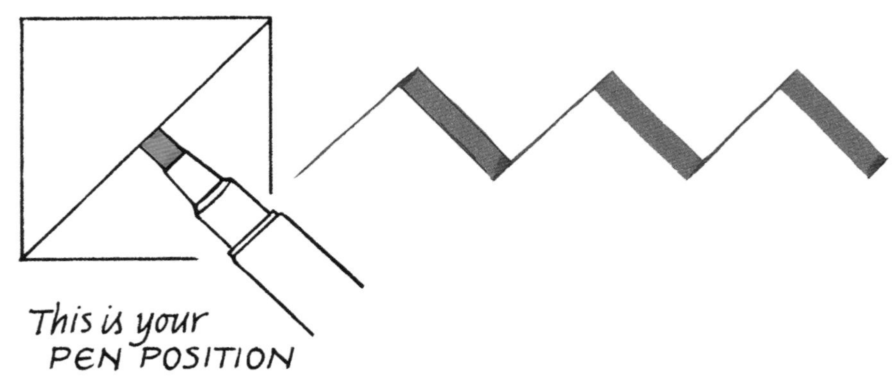

We're going to start with some basic strokes, and then we'll make letters.

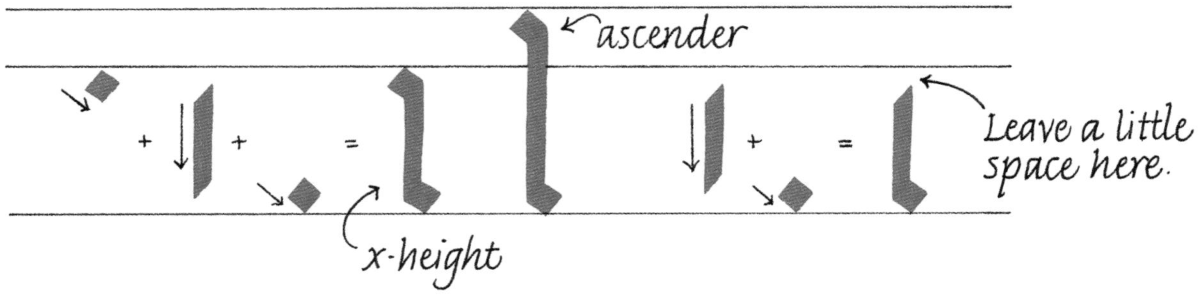

Leave a little space here.

Now try writing the first stroke a few times, keeping the strokes close together.

1 Basic Rule for Gothic Calligraphy

The space between strokes is almost the same as the width of the stroke itself. It is a tiny bit wider.

If you can do this spacing correctly, you will find Gothic calligraphy very easy to learn.

Now let's try some letters. (The finished letters are purple.)

The **o, a, i, l,** and **c.**

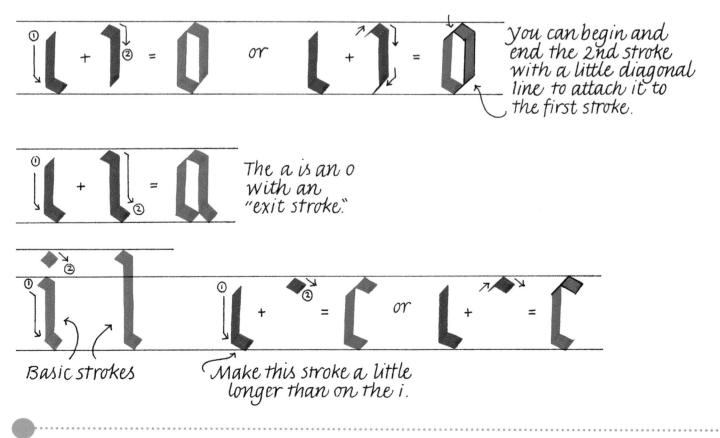

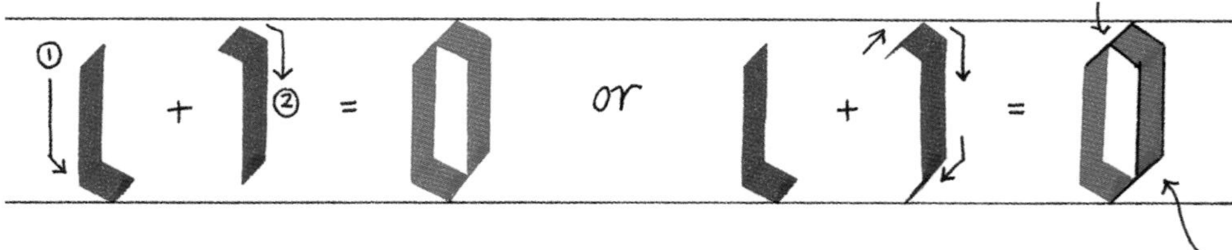

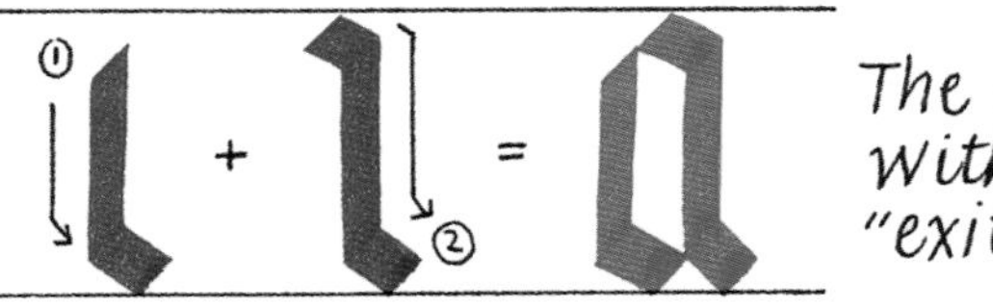

You can begin and end the 2nd stroke with a little diagonal line to attach it to the first stroke.

The a is an o with an "exit stroke."

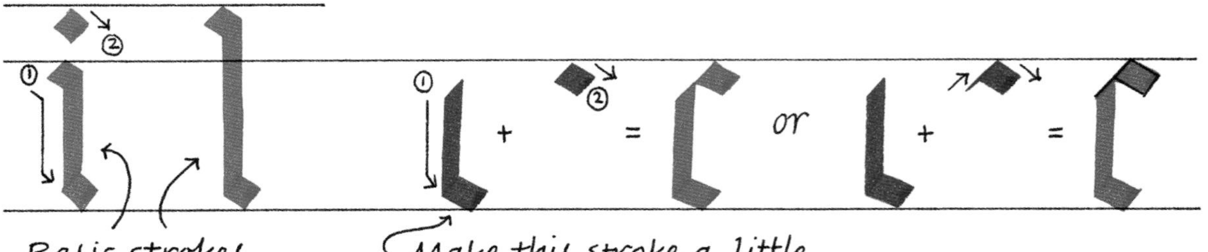

The **b, h, m, n, r, u, v, q,** and **w** are made basically the same way.

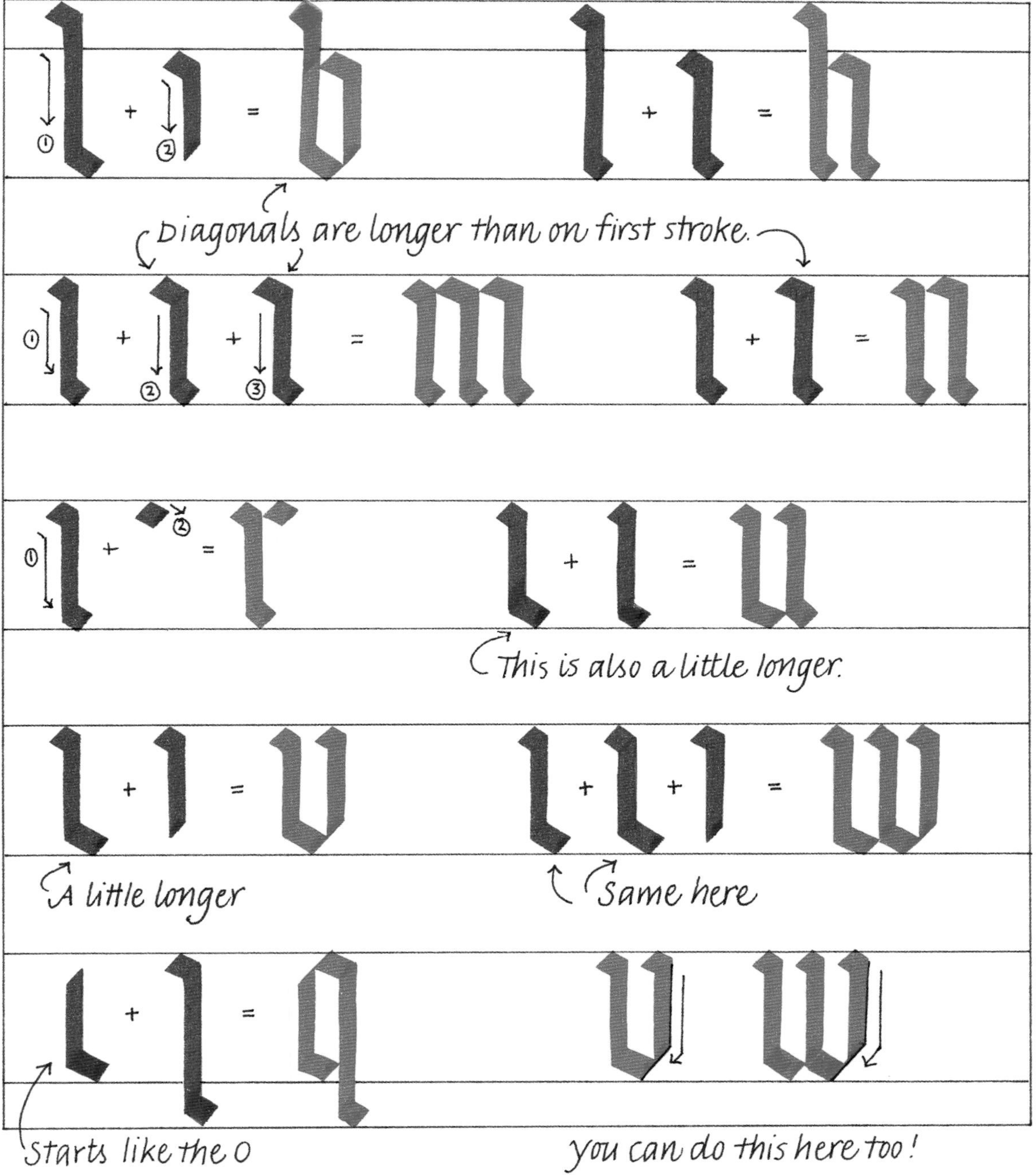

+
=
Diagonals are longer than on first stroke.
This is also a little longer.
A little longer
Same here
Starts like the o
you can do this here too!

The other lowercase letters have some extra strokes or little variations. Here are the **d, e, t, f, j, k, p.**

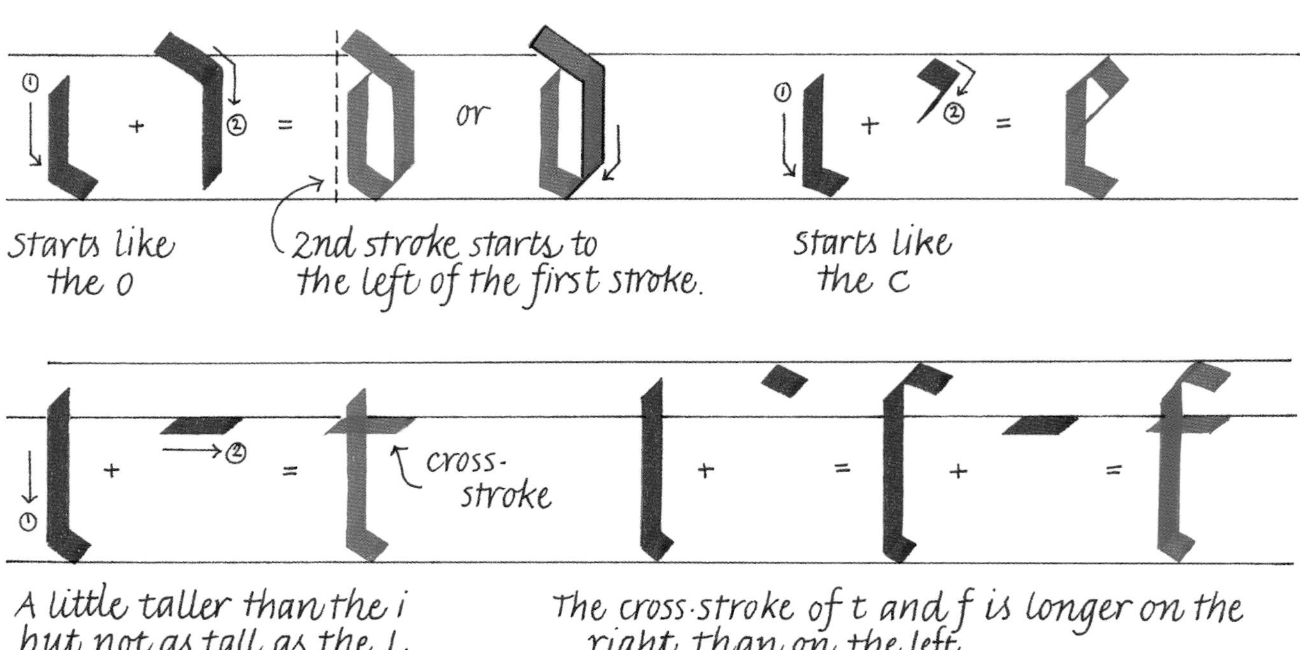

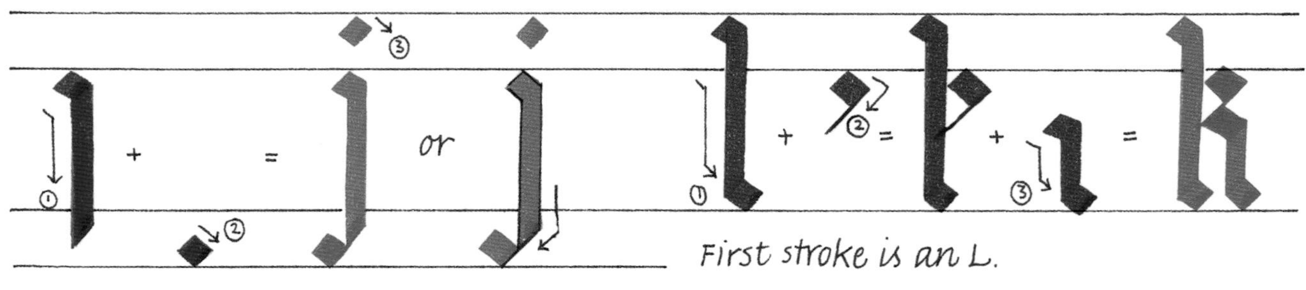

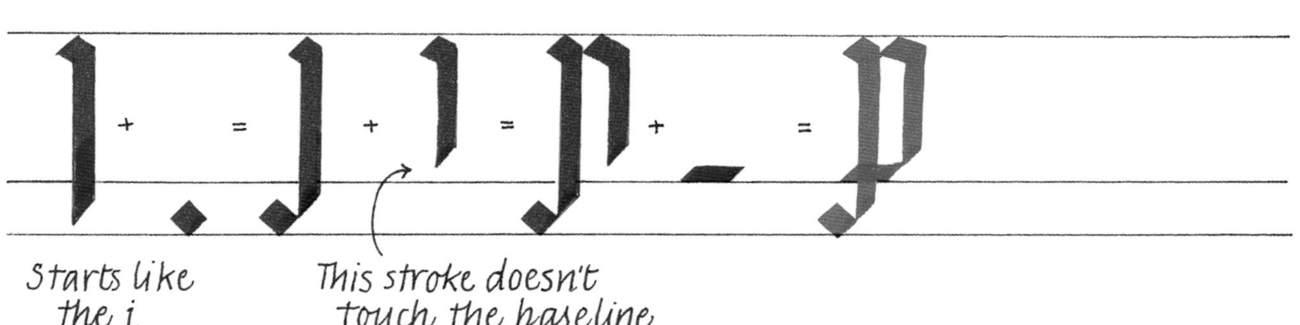

Here are the **x** and **z.**

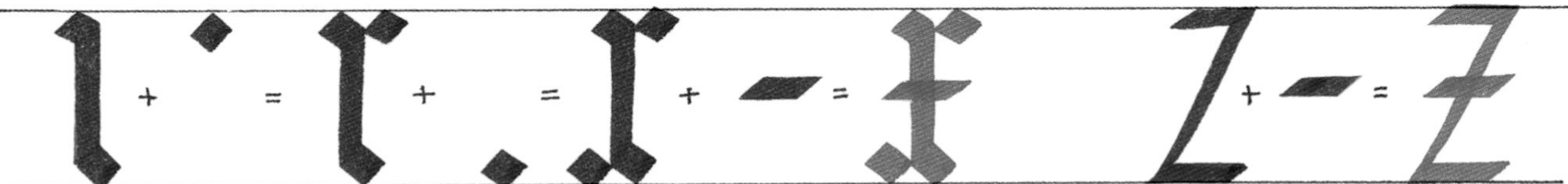

The **g** and **y** are almost alike.

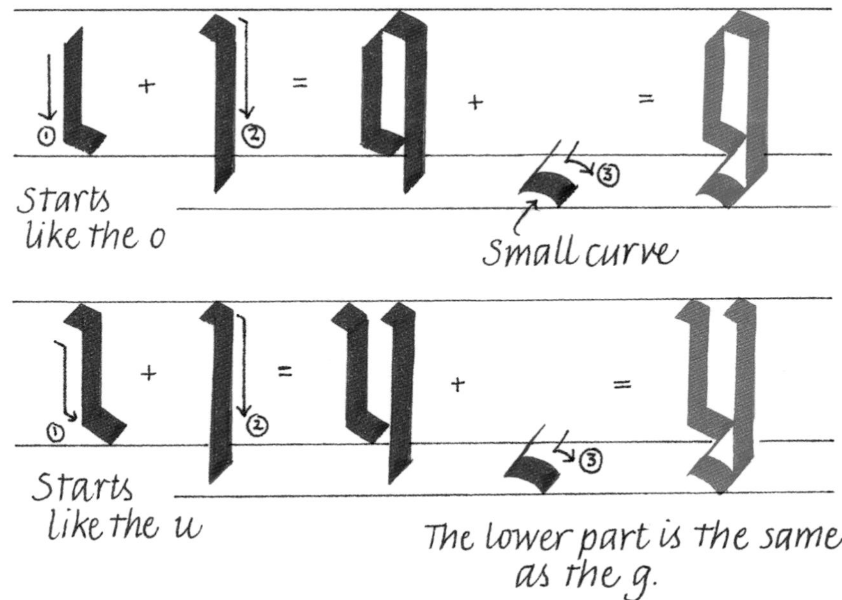
Starts
like the o
Small curve
Starts
like the u
The lower part is the same
as the g.

The **s** is a little different.

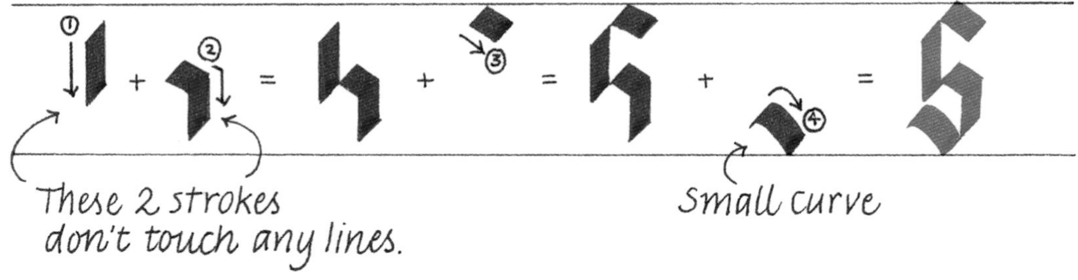
These 2 strokes
don't touch any lines.
Small curve

Here are a few extra letters you can try. These are variations on the ones you just learned.

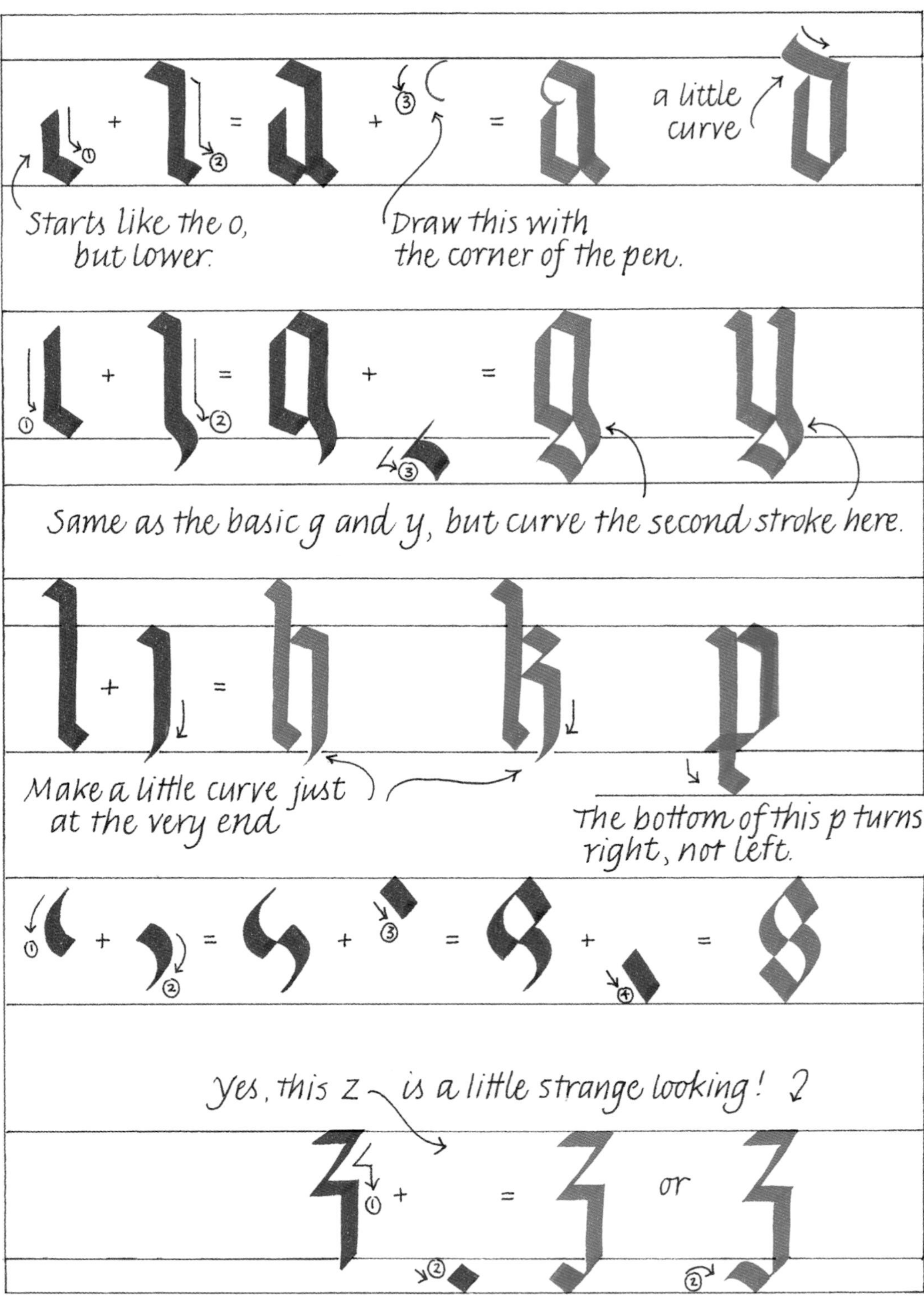

a little curve
Starts like the o, but lower.
Draw this with the corner of the pen.
Same as the basic g and y, but curve the second stroke here.
Make a little curve just at the very end
The bottom of this p turns right, not left.
yes, this z is a little strange looking!
or

Try the Gothic letters with your fountain pen. Take out the guide lines labeled **Gothic #2** and put them under your writing paper. Make each of the letters a few times until they start to feel natural.

Now let's practice **spacing.** Remember the rule. ***Spacing Rule*** When making words, the space between letters appears to be about the same as the space inside the letters.

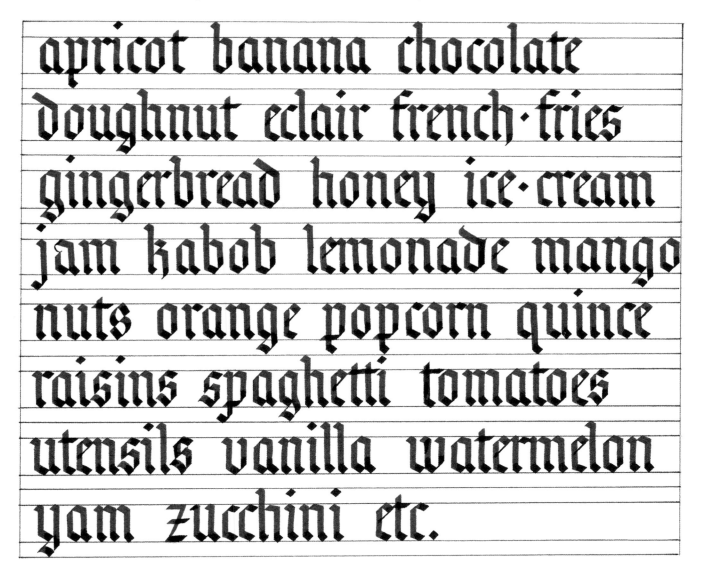

apricot banana chocolate
doughnut eclair french·fries
gingerbread honey ice·cream
jam kabob lemonade mango
nuts orange popcorn quince
raisins spaghetti tomatoes
utensils vanilla watermelon
yam zucchini etc.

In the case of Gothic, the space inside the letters is almost the same size—just a little bigger—than the strokes. So the space between letters will also be the same. Try copying these words, using your fountain pen. In some of the words, letter variations were used in addition to the basic Gothic alphabet.

Here's a short poem you can try copying.

there was an old man of peru,
who dreamed he was
eating his shoe.
he awoke in the night,
in a horrible fright,
and found it was perfectly true.

REMEMBER
Don't write too fast!

9

Gothic Calligraphy

Capital Letters

There are so many Gothic capitals that it's hard to know which ones to choose! Unlike the minuscules, which are fairly standard forms, the scribes in the Middle Ages often invented their own capital letters. Sometimes they were so decorative that we can hardly read them. Often they were drawn and painted with wonderful illustrations of people, animals, plants, and magical beasts inside and outside the letters.

The capitals that we are going to learn are relatively simple. You will be able to make them with your pen or marker, and they will all be recognizable as letters.

The capitals are a little shorter than the lowercase Gothic **h** or **k**. They don't touch the top (ascender) line. If you are working with your marker, be sure to use the **Gothic #1** guide lines. If you are using the fountain pen, the guide lines are **Gothic #2.**

BASIC STROKES

Here are some basic strokes. You can also add **beaks and claws** as well as **decorative strokes** that go near the top of capitals.

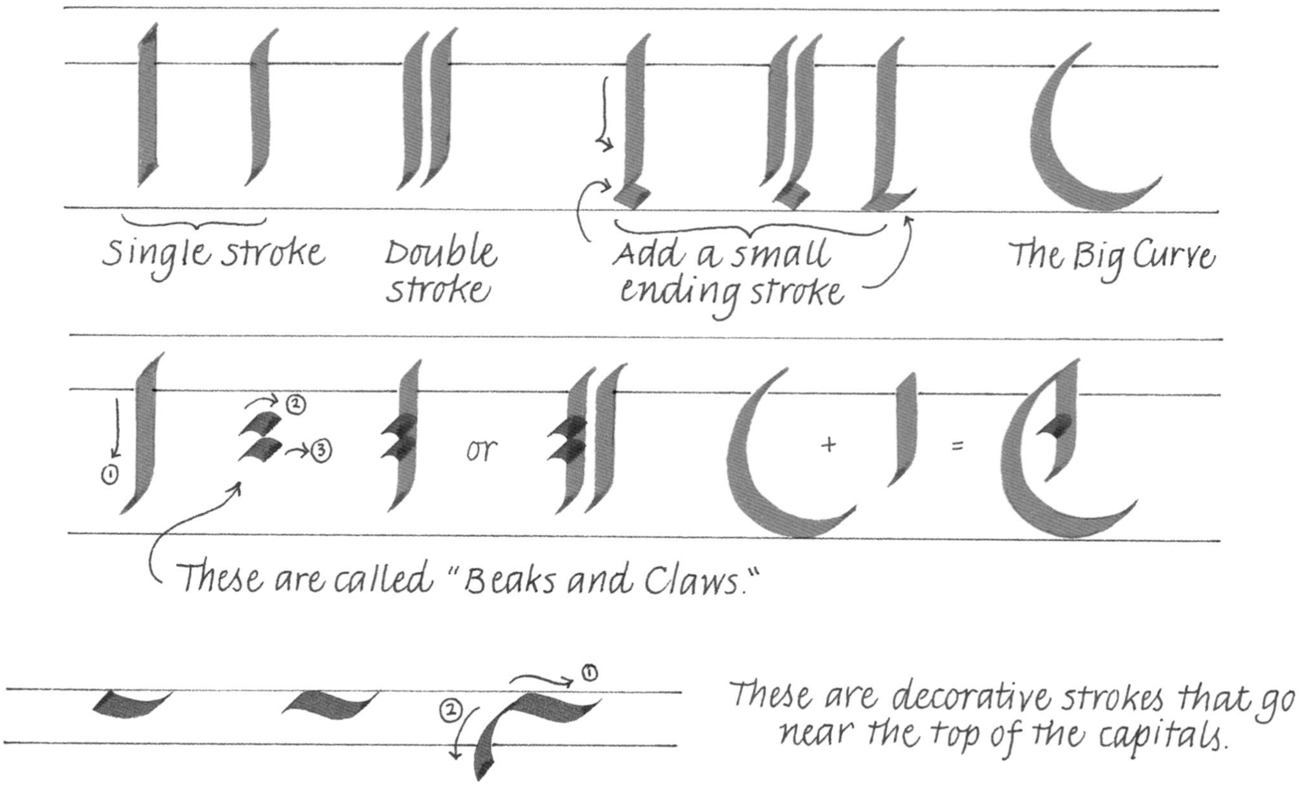

The Double-Stroke Letters

These are the **A and B.**

The double stroke is always first.
Add the decorative strokes last.

Here are **D, E, F, H, I, J, K, L, M, N, P, R, T, U, V, W,** and **Y**.

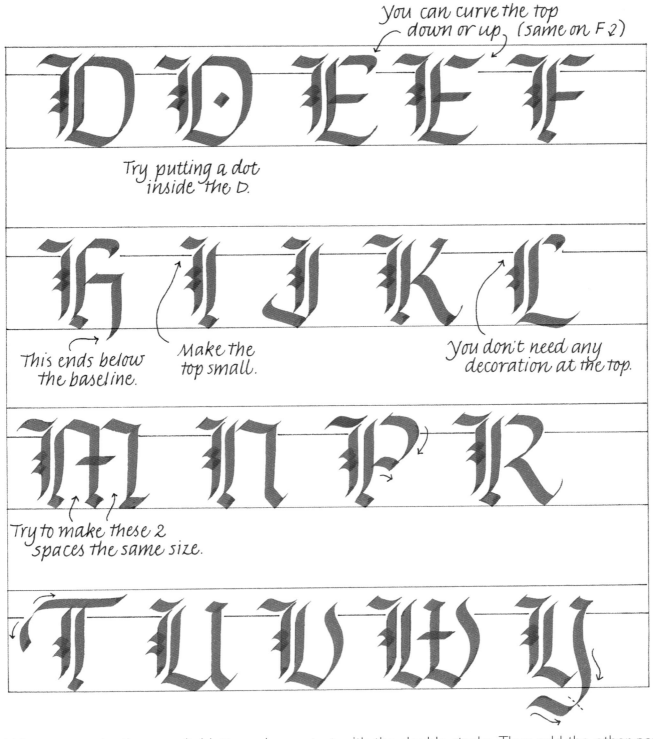

You can curve the top down or up. (same on F 2)

Try putting a dot inside the D.

This ends below the baseline.

Make the top small.

You don't need any decoration at the top.

Try to make these 2 spaces the same size.

When you make these capital letters, always start with the double stroke. Then add the other parts. Put the decorative strokes in last.

The Big-Curve Letters

These are the **C, E, G, O, Q,** and **T**.

The **big curve** is the first stroke of this group of letters.

Notice that the **E** and the **T** appear twice—as double-stroke letters and as big-curve letters. In fact, there are lots of ways to make all the Gothic capital letters.

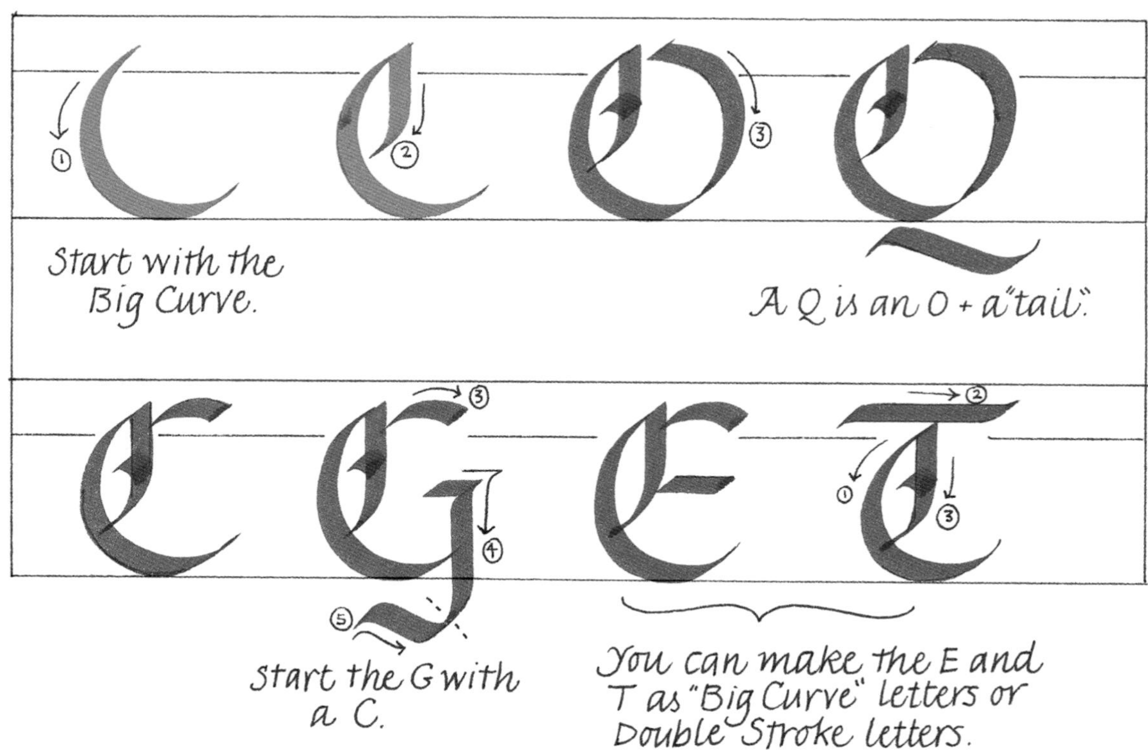

A Q is an O + a "tail."
Start the G with a C.

The Others

The letters **S, X,** and **Z** are made in their own way.

You can make the **S** three different ways. The letters **X** and **Z** are at the top of the next page.

Here are 3 possibilities
The top of this S can curve up or down.

Here are the letters **X** and **Z**.

+
=
+
=
Try to overlap these
2 strokes in the middle.
The middle stroke of the Z
can be single or double.

Extra Ornaments

Add a few extra ornaments if you like. Try double-stroke flourishes, extra beaks and claws, or a dot with extending hairlines.

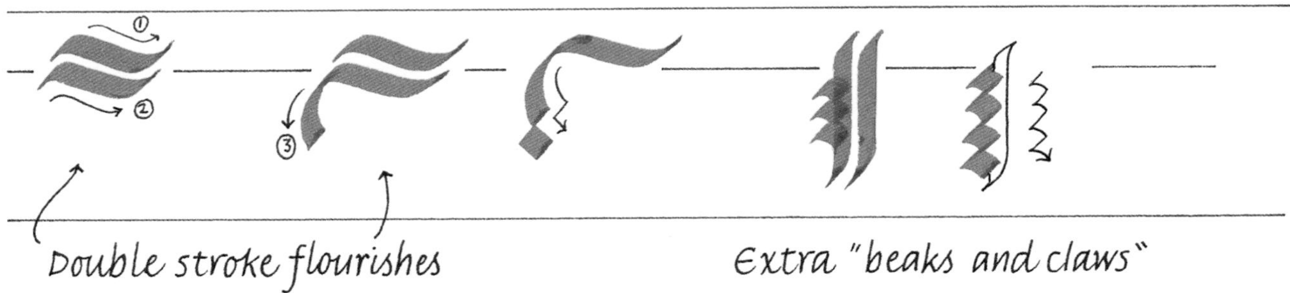

Extra Ornaments

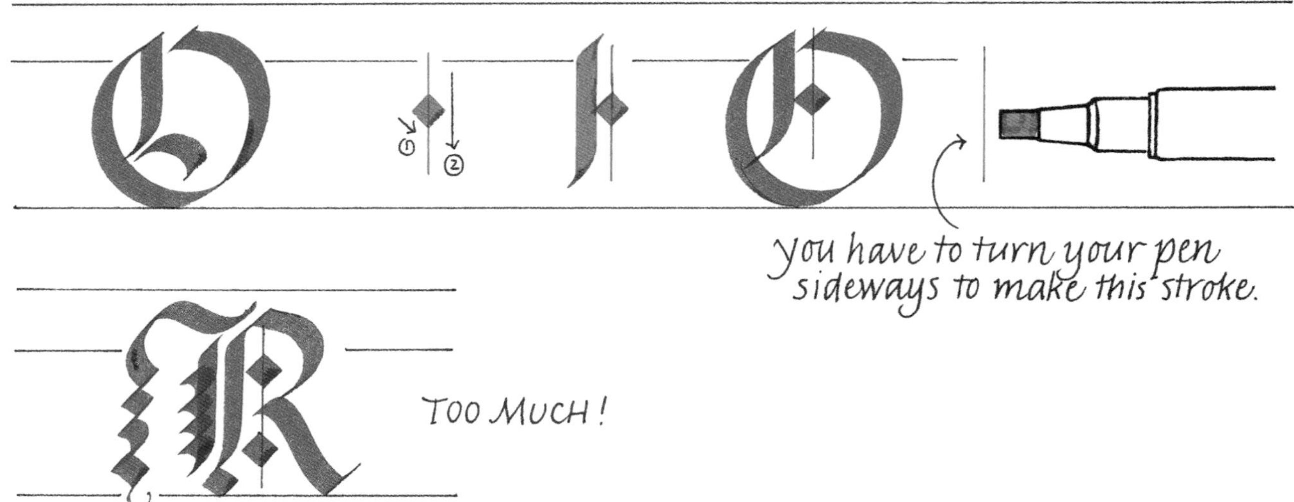

you have to turn your pen sideways to make this stroke.
TOO MUCH!

There are lots of other Gothic capitals you can try. If you look at other calligraphy books (in the library or in bookstores), you will find many variations on every letter in the alphabet. When copying these letters, keep in mind that most of them start on the left with a basic downstroke or a big curve. All the little ornaments are added after you have made the basic letter.

2 Basic Rule of Gothic Calligraphy

Never write a word in all Gothic capitals.

Here's why.

IT CAN BE VERY DIFFICULT TO READ

PRACTICE

A good way to practice the Gothic capitals along with the lowercase letters is to try to come up with a name of a person or a place for each letter of the alphabet. Or you could try something different like fruit and vegetables. Any words at all will do, as long as the first letter is a capital and the rest are lowercase. See if you can find long words to practice. That way you can work on your spacing at the same time you practice the letters.

Don't write too fast!

Try copying these words and then make your own list. These were written with a fountain pen.

Zimbabwe Yemen Xebec
Wisconsin Venice Uruguay
Trinidad Saskatchewan
Romania Queensland
Philadelphia Oslo Nigeria
Marakesh London Kenya
Jerusalem Ireland Honduras
Ghana Finland Egypt Devon
California Belgium Algeria

10

Uncial Calligraphy

Uncial (pronounced "UN-shull," with the emphasis on the first syllable) is a very old alphabet. It was used as a bookhand (to make books) 1,500 years ago. There was no uppercase and lowercase then, just one group of letters that served both purposes. So for Uncial we only need to learn 26 letters, not 52 like Italic or Gothic.

You will see that some of the Uncial letters look like capitals, some look like lowercase, and some like a mixture of the two.

Historical Note When Uncial was in use, there were fewer letters in the alphabet. There was no **j, v,** or **w.** The **i** was used for both **i** and **j,** and the **u** was used instead of the **v.** The **w** was a double-**u.** Modern calligraphers have added these letters to the Uncial alphabet in shapes that match the rest of the letters.

A NEW PEN POSITION

For the next two alphabets, **Uncial** and **Roman,** we are going to change the pen position—or pen angle—so that the relationship between the edge of the pen or marker and the baseline will be different.

The new pen position is also called a 30° (30-degree) pen angle. Once again, we are giving you the mathematical term, 30° pen angle, but the important thing is what it looks like, not what we call it. For our purposes, let's just call it the **flattened pen position.**

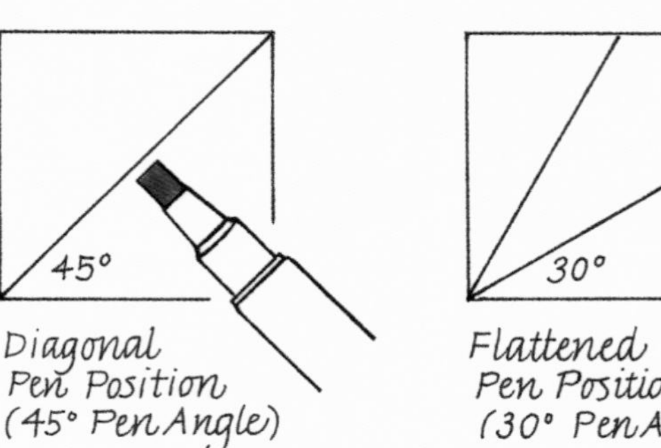

EXERCISE

Using guide lines labeled **Pen Exercises** (the same guide lines we started with in Chapter 5), make some more zigzags. With your pen or marker in the flattened pen position, the lines will look like this.

Make a few lines of these zigzags until your pen feels comfortable.

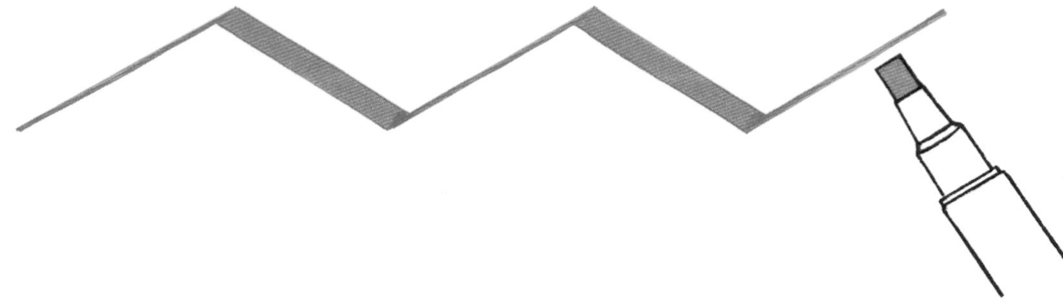

Now try some vertical lines, some horizontal lines, and some crosses.

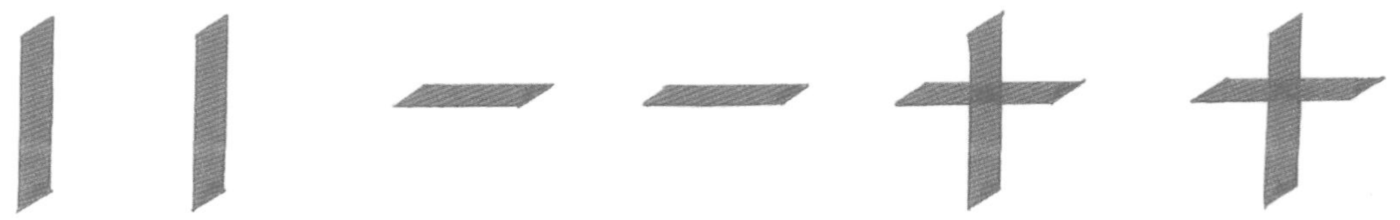

With your pen in the flattened pen position (30° angle), the downstroke of the cross is thicker than the stroke going from left to right. Making crosses is a good way to check your pen position.

Diagonal Pen Position

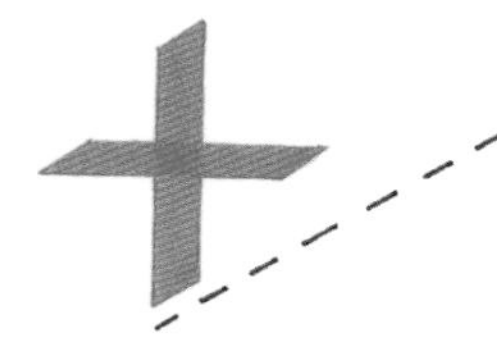

Flattened Pen Position

OK. Now let's learn Uncial.

We're going to start with our pencil or pointed marker, as we did for Italic, in order to try the skeleton forms of the alphabet. Take out the **Uncial #1** guide lines, and put them under your paper.

Here are the skeleton forms, the "bones" of the Uncial alphabet.

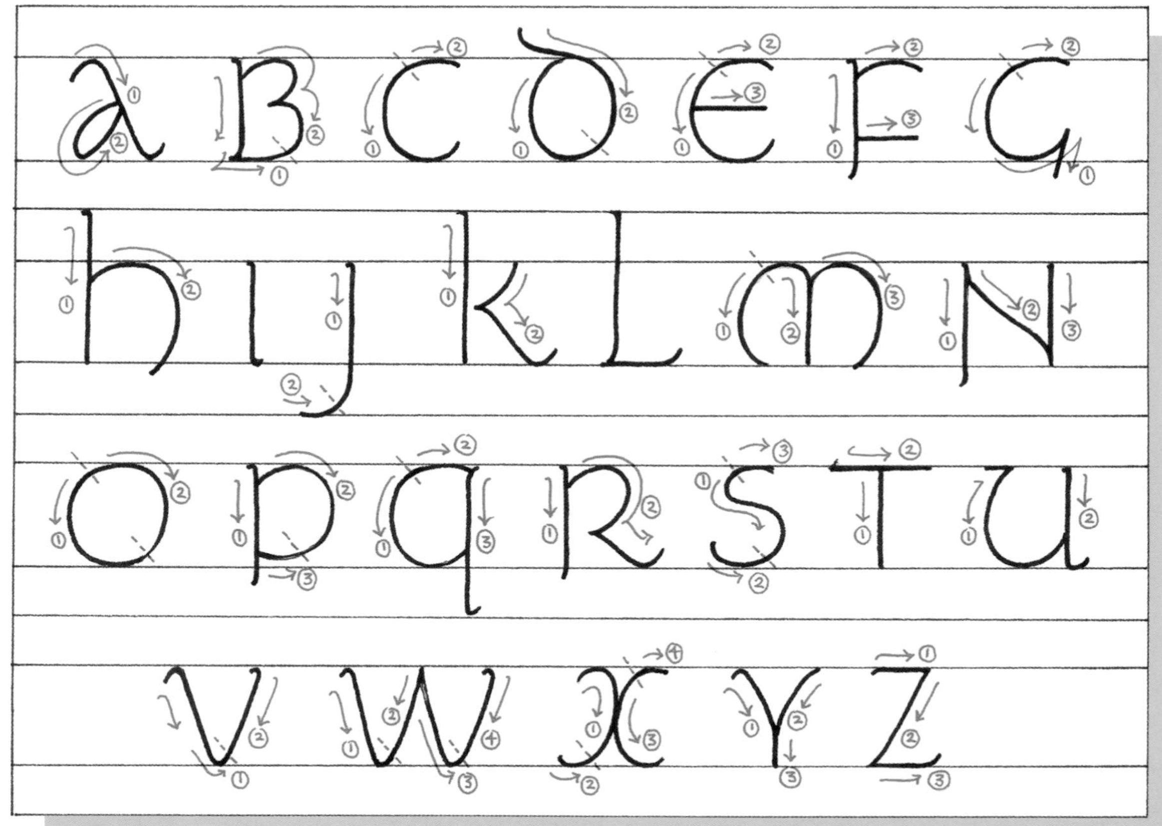

Try to make these letters slowly, following the order of the strokes shown above.

We're now going to work with our calligraphy markers, using the same guide lines. First review the flattened pen position (30° pen angle) by making some zigzags and downstrokes.

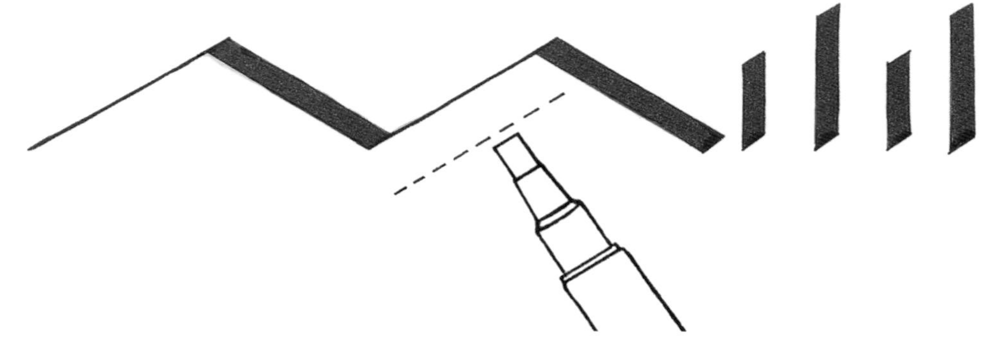

Now add a very small beginning and ending stroke to the downstrokes.

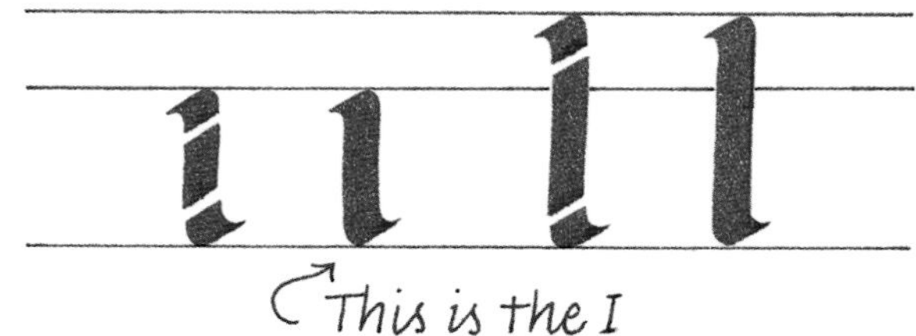
This is the I

Don't make these strokes too quickly, or they may look like this.

Good news! You've just made an i! It has no dot.

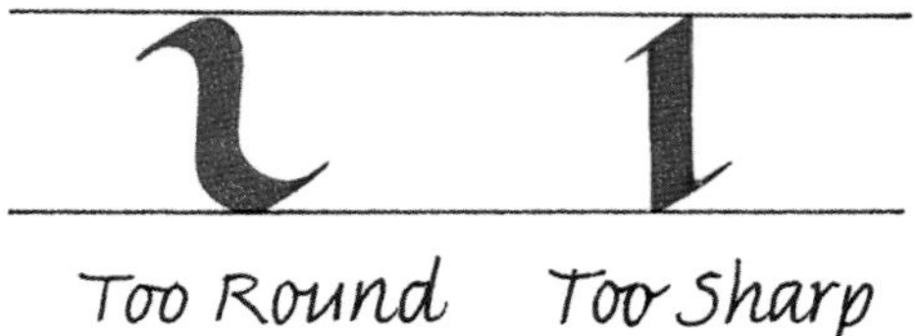
Too Round
Too Sharp

As we did in Italic, we'll begin with the straight letters. You already made an **i,** so let's continue with **j, l,** and **t.**

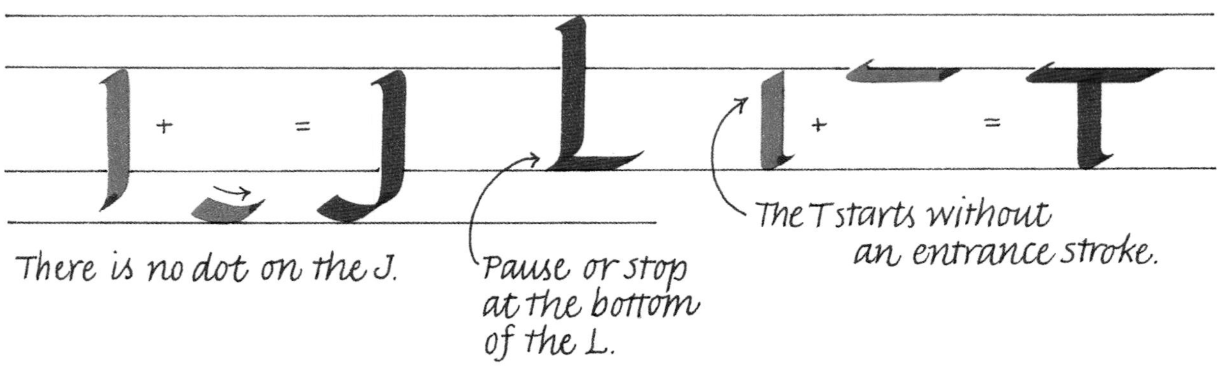
There is no dot on the J.
Pause or stop at the bottom of the L.
The T starts without an entrance stroke.

Notice that the descender (the bottom) of the **j** and the ascender (the top) of the **l** are only a little longer than the x-height (the main part of the letter). This is one reason that Uncial looks a bit like a combination of capitals and lowercase letters.

Our next group is the round letters, or letters that are partly round. They are the **o, c, e, g, q, d, h, u, m,** and **p.**

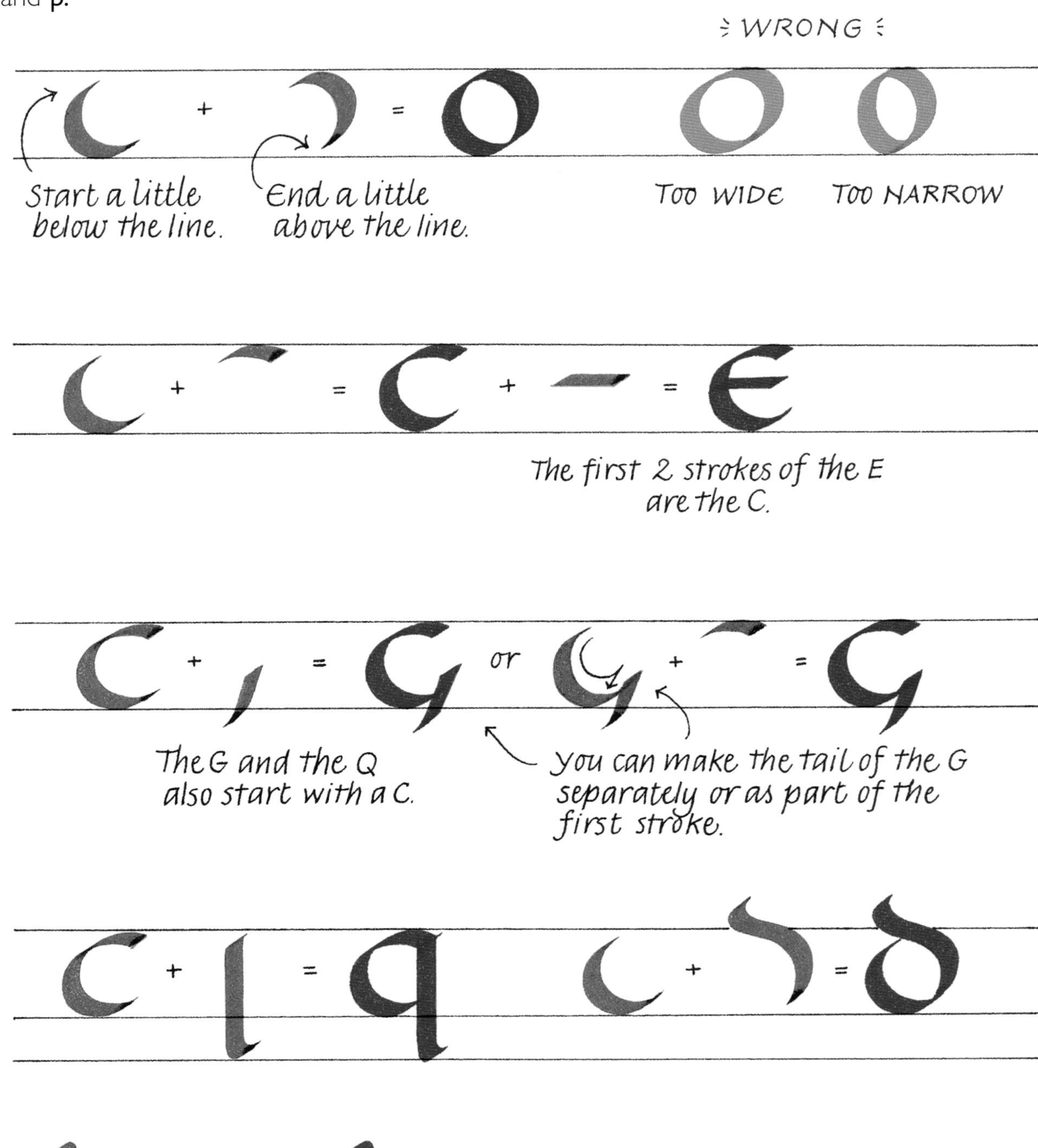
WRONG
Start a little below the line.
End a little above the line.
TOO WIDE
TOO NARROW
The first 2 strokes of the E are the C.
or
The G and the Q also start with a C.
You can make the tail of the G separately or as part of the first stroke.
The H ends a little below the line.

This group of letters, the **b, f, k, n,** and **r,** starts with a straight line, like the **i** or the **l.**

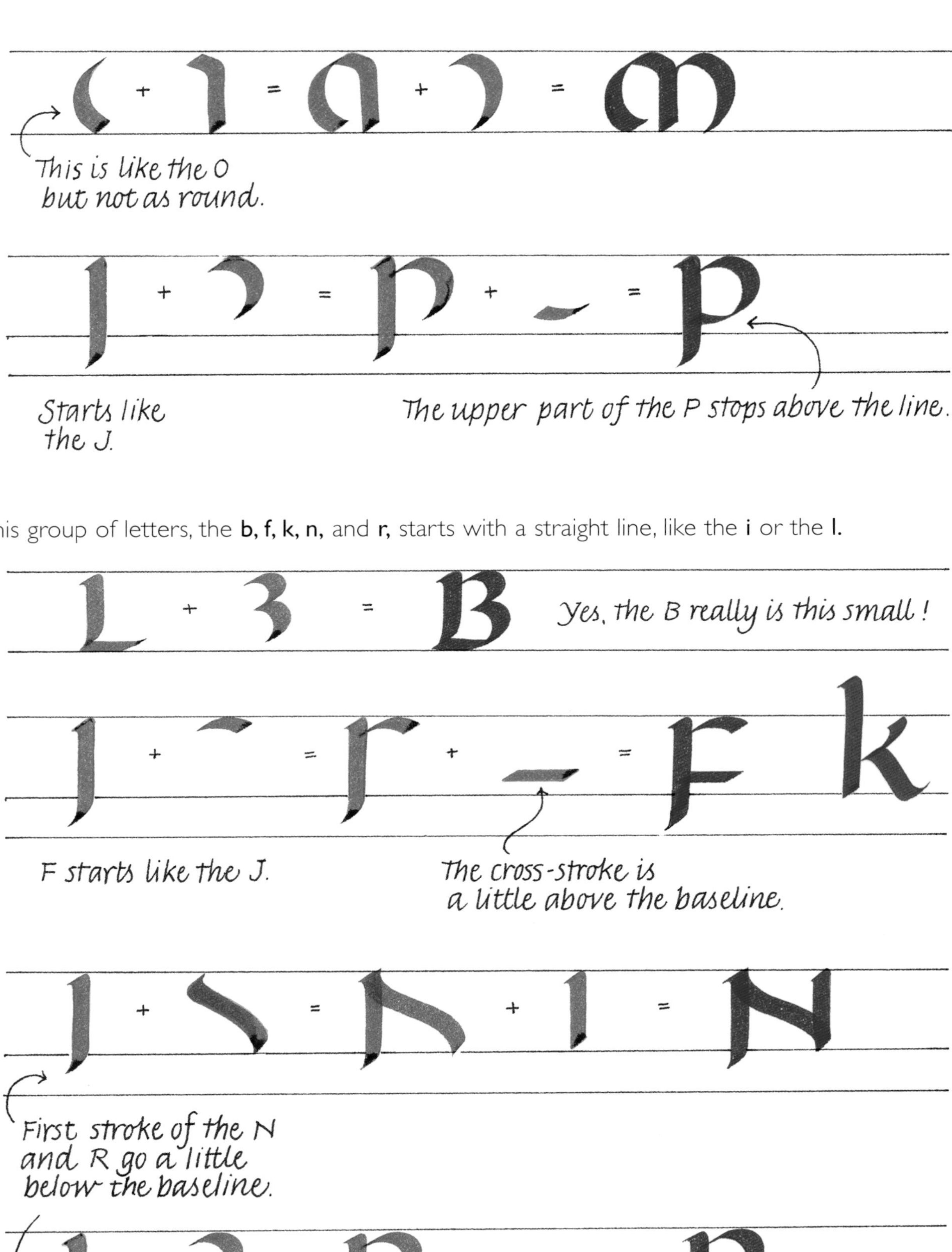

This is like the O
but not as round.
Starts like
the J.
The upper part of the P stops above the line.
Yes, the B really is this small!
F starts like the J.
The cross-stroke is
a little above the baseline.
First stroke of the N
and R go a little
below the baseline.

The rest of the letters are special cases, the **a, s, v, w, x, y,** and **z.**

+ = + =

The first stroke of the A is almost the same as the V and W, but the A is wider:

A → V, W

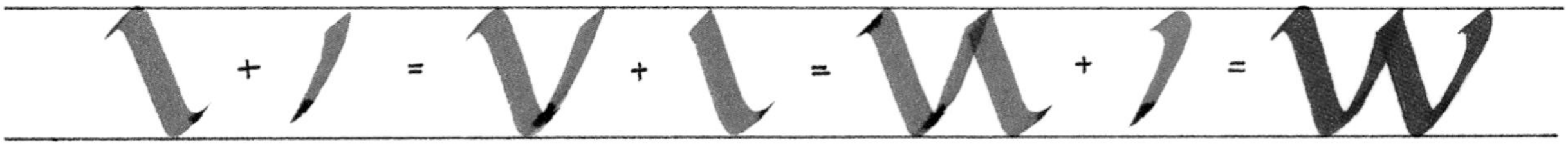

+ = + = + =

The V and W are a little rounded at the baseline (not pointy).

+ = + =

The first stroke of the S is the center stroke.

Make the bottom stroke next, the top last.

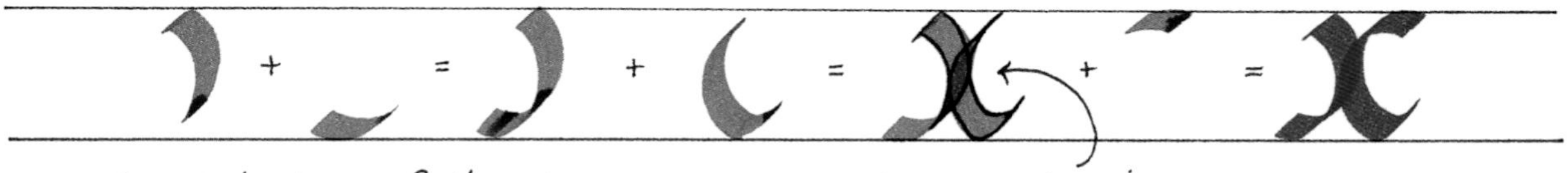

+ = + = + =

The 2 halves of the X go in opposite directions

They overlap in the middle (like the Gothic capital X)

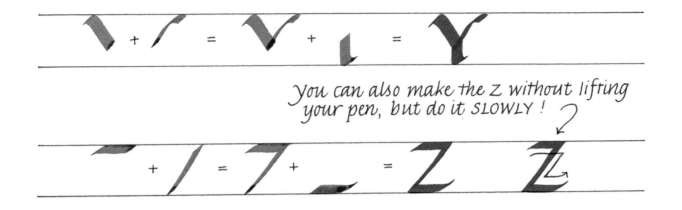

You can also make the Z without lifting your pen, but do it SLOWLY !

A few Uncial letters may look a little unusual to you, such as the **g, m, n,** and **x,** but they are easy to read when you make words.

Try the Uncial alphabet with your fountain pen, using the **Uncial #2** guide lines, and then we'll try some words.

SPACING

Spacing with Uncials is a little harder than with Italic or Gothic letters. That's because some letters are very straight and narrow and some are very round. We still follow the spacing rule, but because many Uncial letters are wide and have a lot of white space inside them, we have to leave more space around all the letters when we make words than we do with the other alphabets.

This is probably easier to see than to imagine.

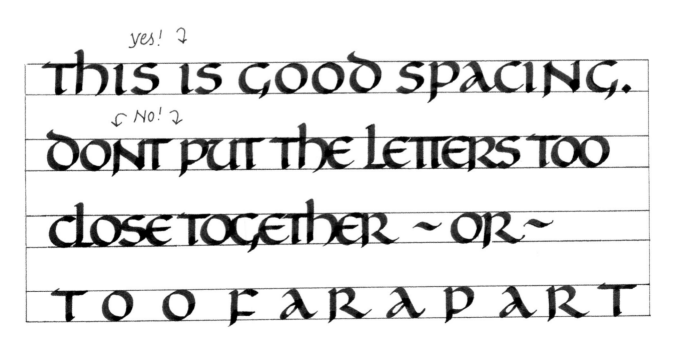

yes!

THIS IS GOOD SPACING.

No!

DONT PUT THE LETTERS TOO CLOSE TOGETHER ~ OR ~

T O O F A R A P A R T

How to Practice Write some words in Uncial. Using a colored pencil or a colored pointed marker, fill in the spaces inside the letters and between the letters, like this.

BIRTHDAY PARTY
HAPPY NEW YEAR

You should have about the same amount of color "inside" and "outside" the letters. This exercise will help you see your mistakes more clearly

WRONG UNEVEN

Here's a paragraph for you to copy. This example was done with a fountain pen, but if you prefer to use your calligraphy marker, remember to use the bigger guide lines (**Uncial #1**).

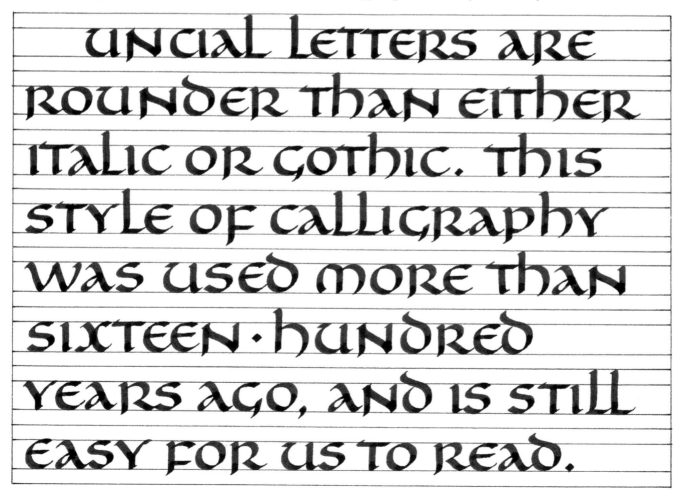

UNCIAL LETTERS ARE
ROUNDER THAN EITHER
ITALIC OR GOTHIC. THIS
STYLE OF CALLIGRAPHY
WAS USED MORE THAN
SIXTEEN · HUNDRED
YEARS AGO, AND IS STILL
EASY FOR US TO READ.

11

Roman Calligraphy

Lowercase (Minuscule) Letters

The Roman alphabet should look very familiar to you. The shapes of the letters are like those we often see printed in books and newspapers. The words *type, typeface,* or *typography* describe these printed letters. Roman letters are also very similar to the first writing we learn in school.

What we call **Roman minuscule** (in this book) has many other names. The basic shape of these letters comes from the Renaissance, around 1400, when it was called Humanist Script or Humanist Bookhand.

Historical Note Italic was originally a handwriting based on this script. Italic developed when the Roman lowercase letters were written faster and narrower. The letters were sometimes connected to each other in order to be written quickly.

But the Roman letters that we're going to learn must be written slowly in order for them to look good. Let's start with our pencils or pointed markers to learn the skeletons of the letters. Use the **Roman #1** guide lines.

Try to copy the letters in the example below.

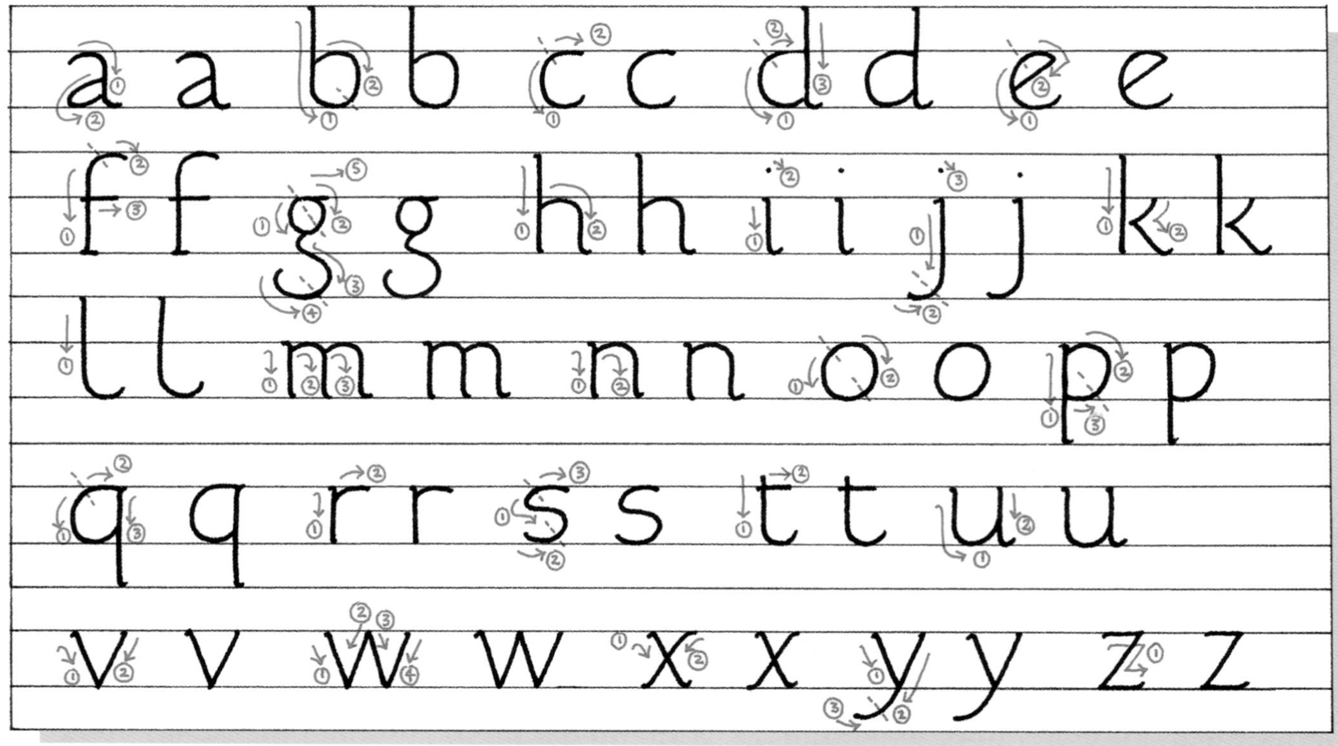

After you have done the skeleton forms, it's time to use your calligraphy markers and the Roman #2 guide lines. Hold your marker in the same position as for Uncial, the flattened pen position (30° pen angle).

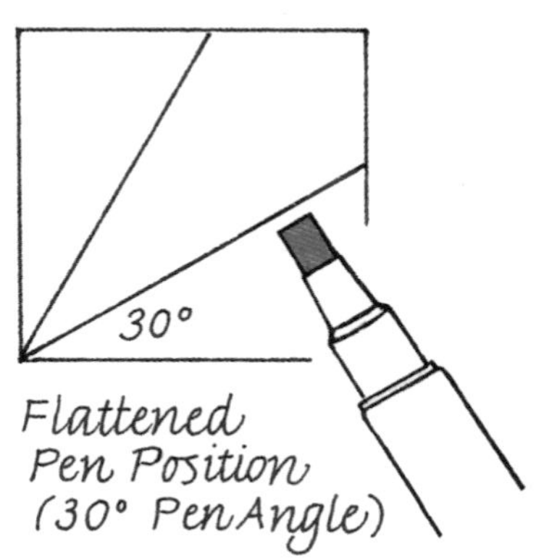

The **basic stroke** is also the same as it is for Uncial.

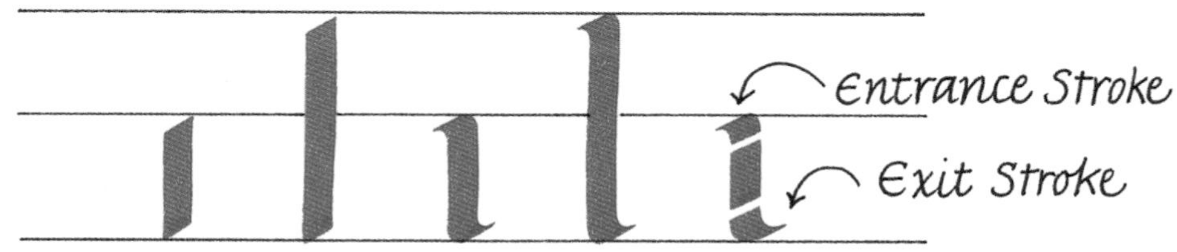

We'll start with the **straight group**. These are the **i, j, t, l,** and **f.**

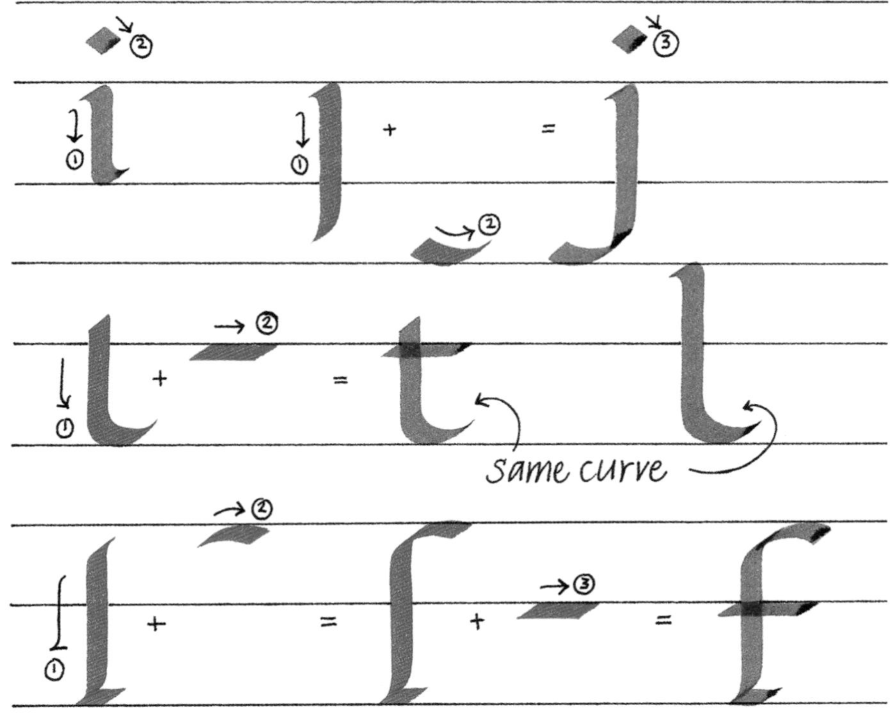

Now let's look at the **o group**. These are the **o, c,** and **e.**

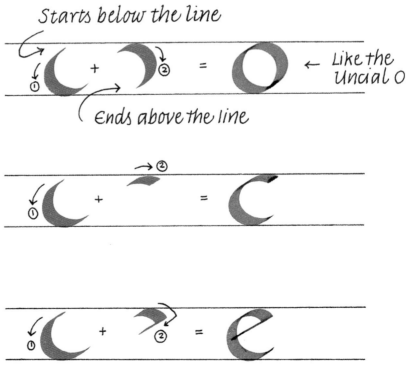

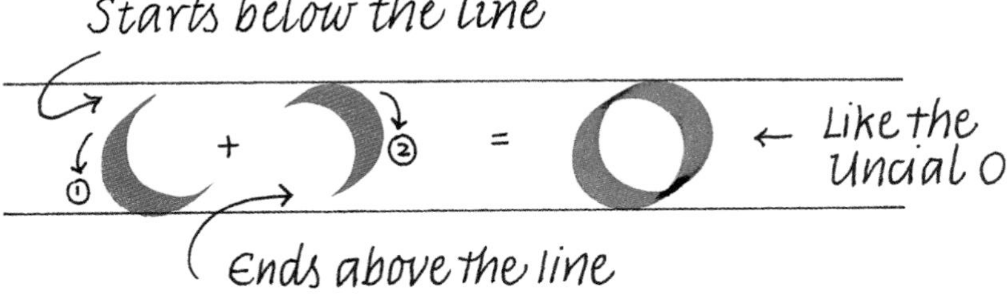

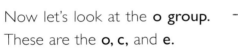

The next group of letters has straight lines and curves. These are the **b, d, h, m, n, p, q, r,** and **u.**

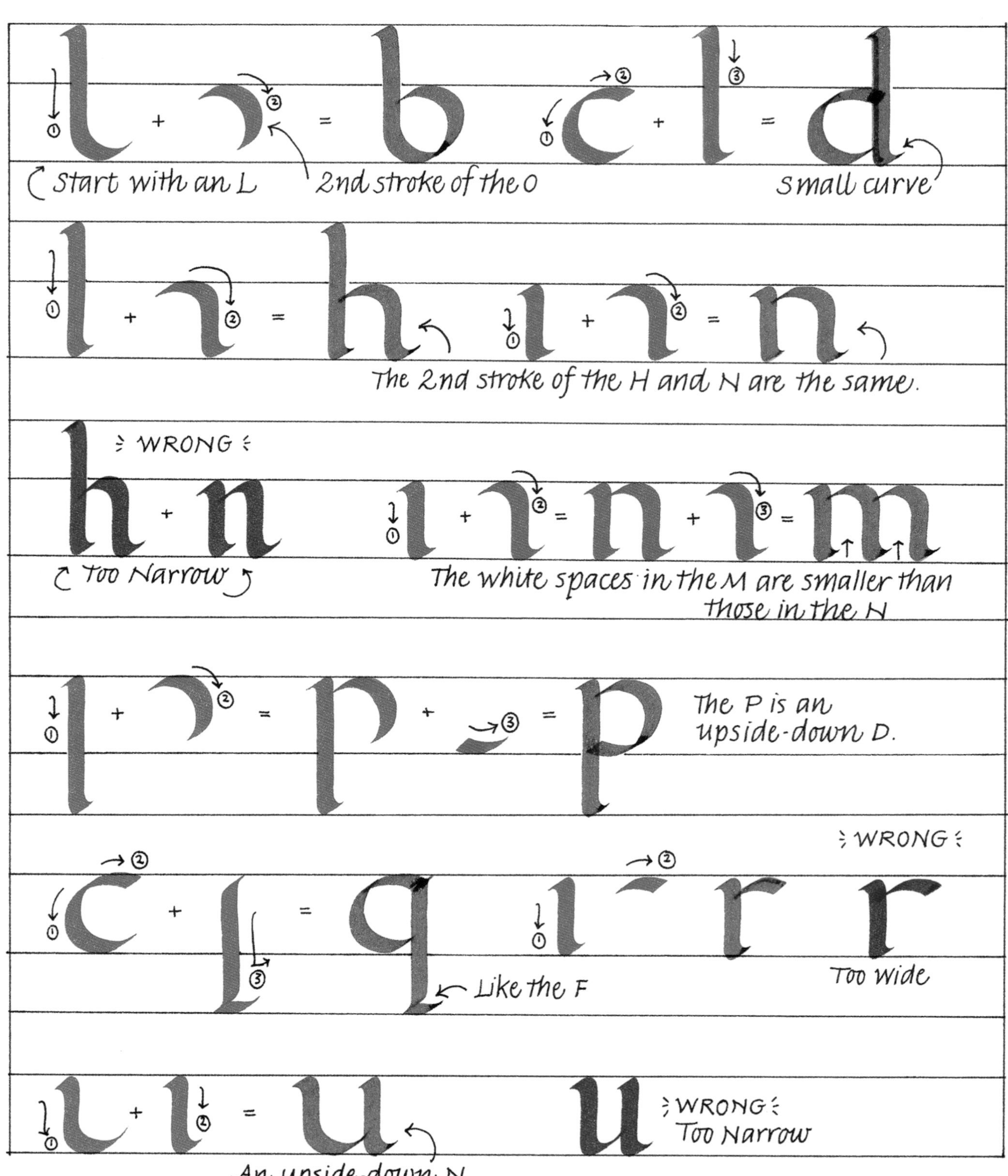
Start with an L
2nd stroke of the O
small curve
The 2nd stroke of the H and N are the same.
WRONG
Too Narrow
The white spaces in the M are smaller than those in the N
The P is an upside-down D.
WRONG
Like the F
Too wide
WRONG
Too Narrow
An upside-down N

And here are the other letters, the **a, g, k, s, v, w, x, y,** and **z.**

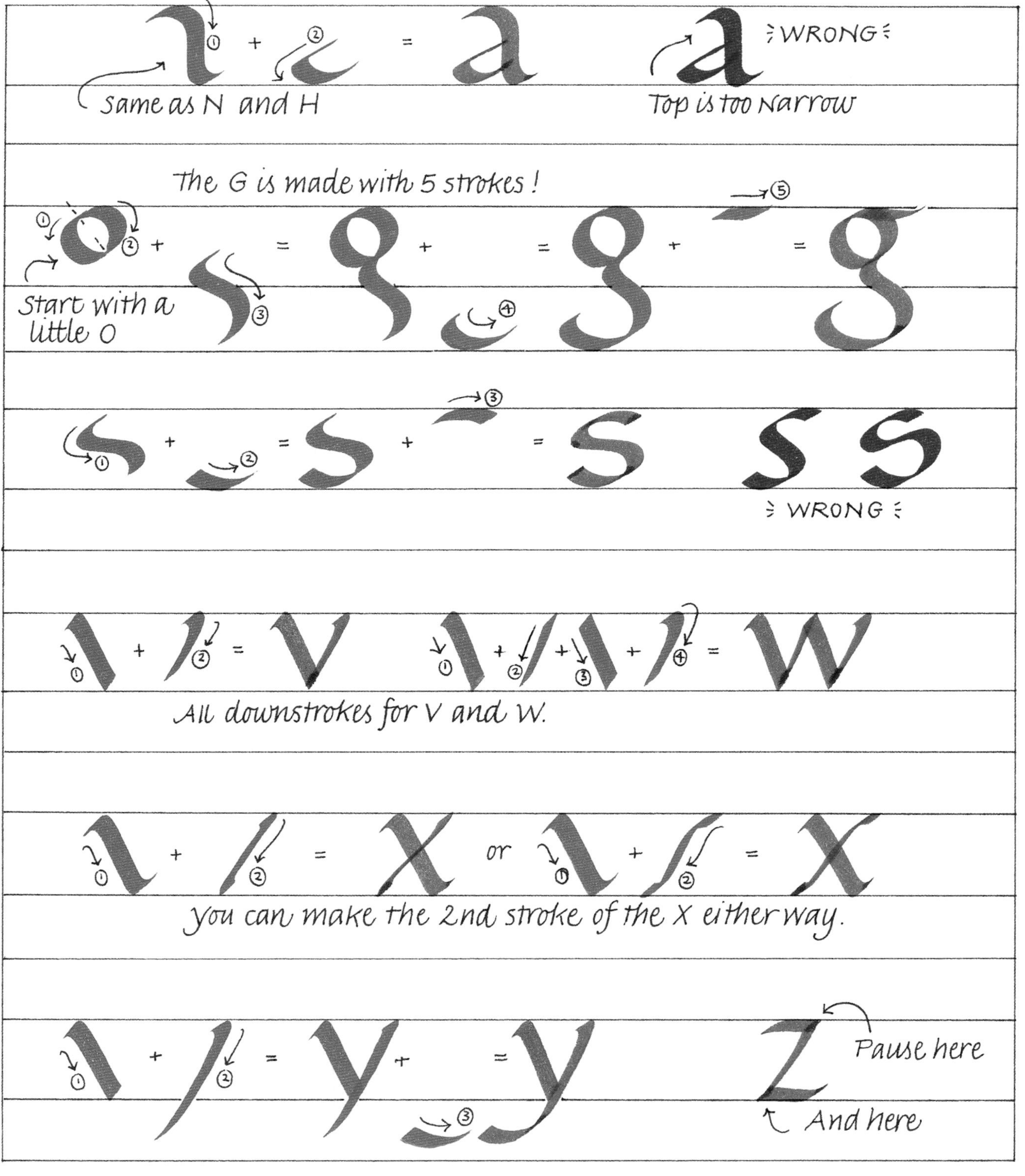

WRONG
Same as N and H
Top is too Narrow
The G is made with 5 strokes!
Start with a little o
WRONG
All downstrokes for V and W.
or
You can make the 2nd stroke of the X either way.
Pause here
And here

SPACING

Spacing Roman lowercase letters is like spacing Uncials because you have some very straight letters and some very round ones. So, like Uncial, it will take a little more practice to get the spacing right than it does for Italic or Gothic.

Let's write some words with our markers before switching to the fountain pen. See page 79.

How to Practice

1. Using your fountain pen (and **Roman #1** guide lines), try the coloring exercise like the one you did in the Uncial chapter. See below.
2. Try writing some sentences in Roman (without capitals).

try this exercise
to practice your
letter spacing

elephant

alphabetical

cucumbers

flowerpot

gymnasium

qualification

12

Roman Calligraphy

Capital Letters

Roman capitals are very easy letters to read. But like a lot of things that look very simple, they are not easy to do well. Give yourself extra time to practice these letters and remember to work *slowly!*

We'll start with the skeleton forms, using our pencils or pointed markers, and the **Roman #1** guide lines. The height of the capitals is the same as the height of the lowercase **b, h, k,** and **l,** so be sure you use two spaces on your guide lines.

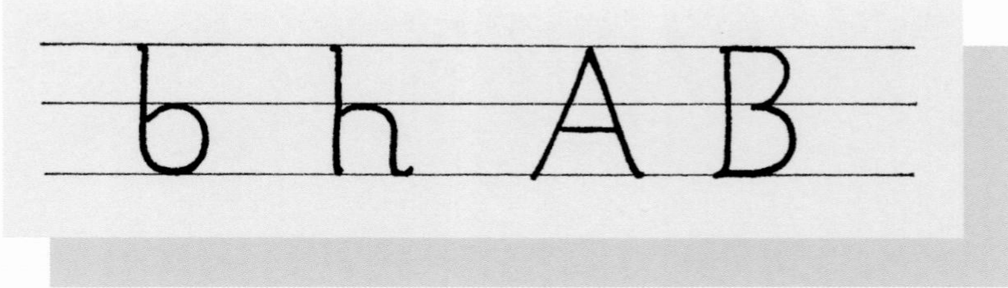

The Roman capitals can be divided into four groups: the round letters, the medium-size letters, the narrow letters, and the extra-wide letters. See next page.

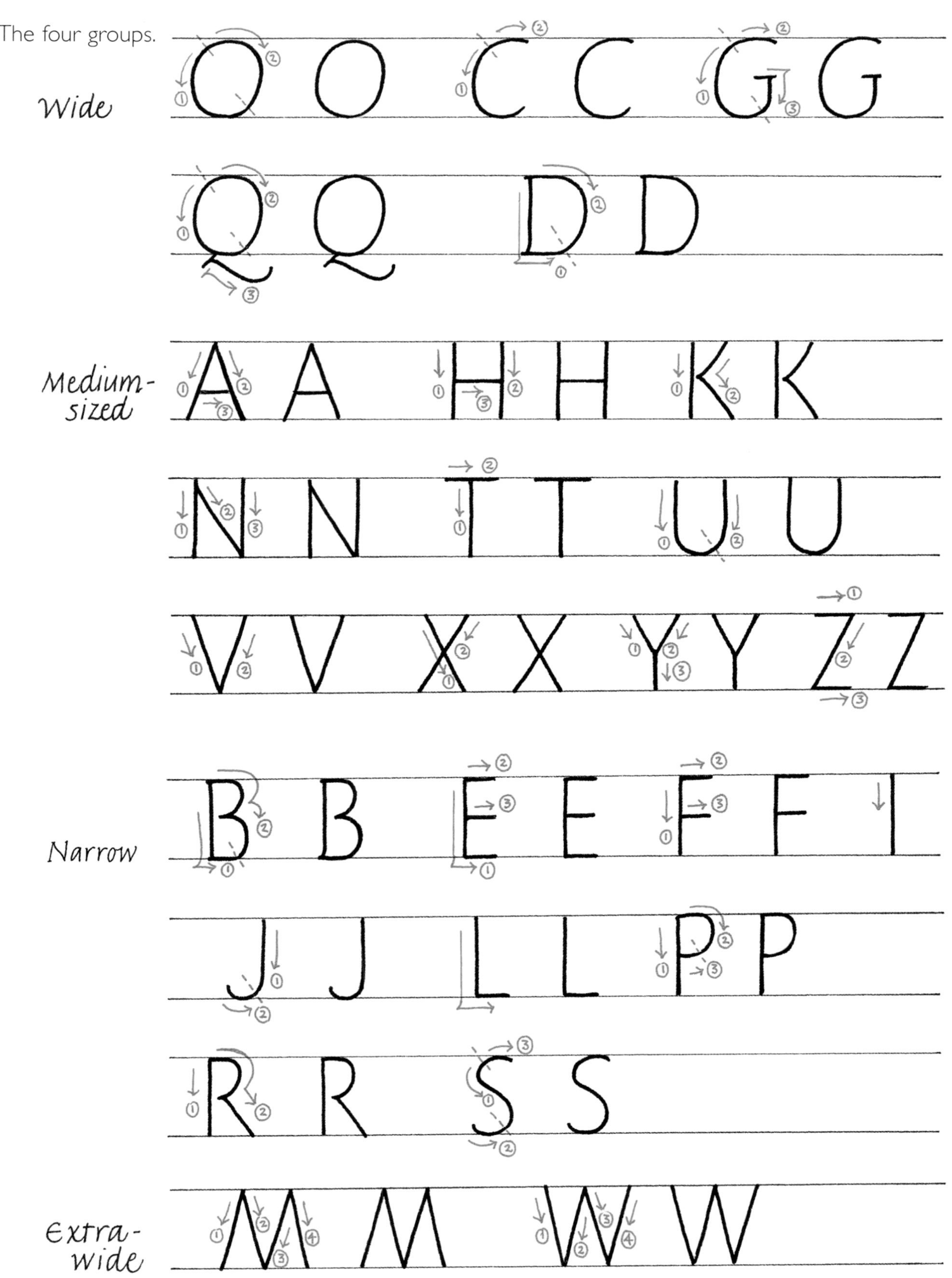

The four groups.

Using your calligraphy markers and **Roman #2** guide lines, let's try these letters in the same groups: round, medium, narrow, and extra wide. Keep the marker in the flattened pen position (30° pen angle), as you do for the lowercase letters. There are a few letters which have a different pen position, but we will show you these exceptions after we try the basic letters.

THE ROUND LETTERS

The round letters are the **O, C, G, Q,** and **D.**

All these letters, with the exception of the **D,** start with the same **big curve.** This curve is like the first stroke of the lowercase Roman **o** and **c,** but considerably taller.

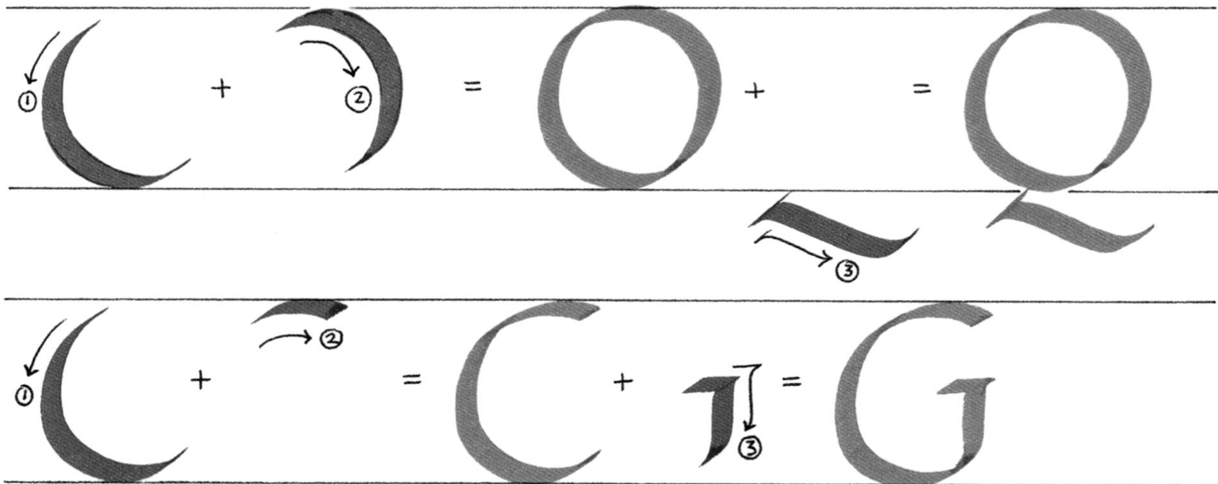

The **D** is also a round letter, even though it starts with a straight line.

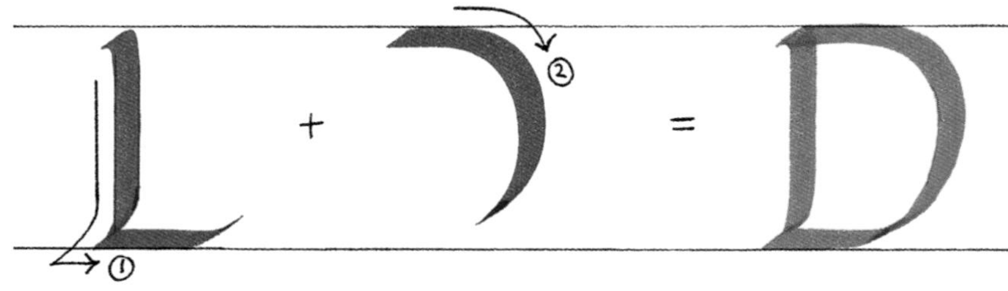

THE MEDIUM-SIZE LETTERS

The medium-size letters are the **A, H, K, N, T, U, V, X, Y,** and **Z.**

We're going to make these letters using the beginning or ending (entrance or exit) strokes that we use in the lowercase Roman letters.

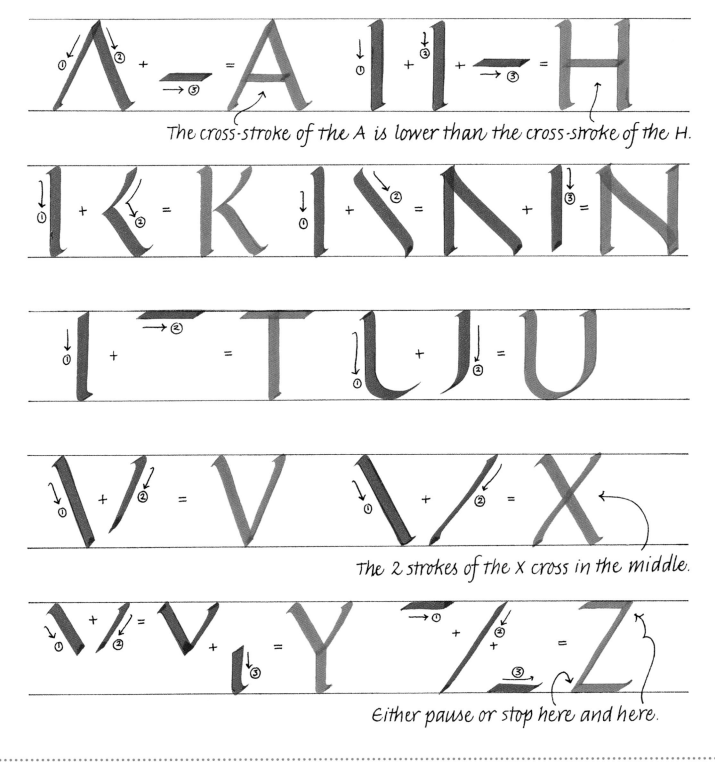

The cross-stroke of the A is lower than the cross-stroke of the H.

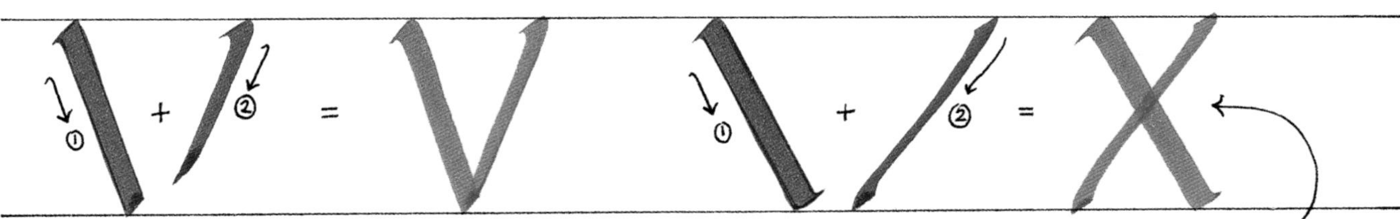

The 2 strokes of the X cross in the middle.

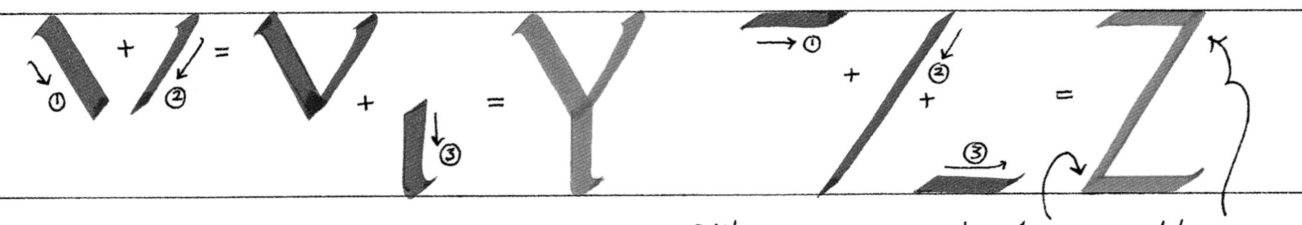

Either pause or stop here and here.

THE NARROW LETTERS

The narrow letters are the **B, E, F, I, J, L, P, R,** and **S.**

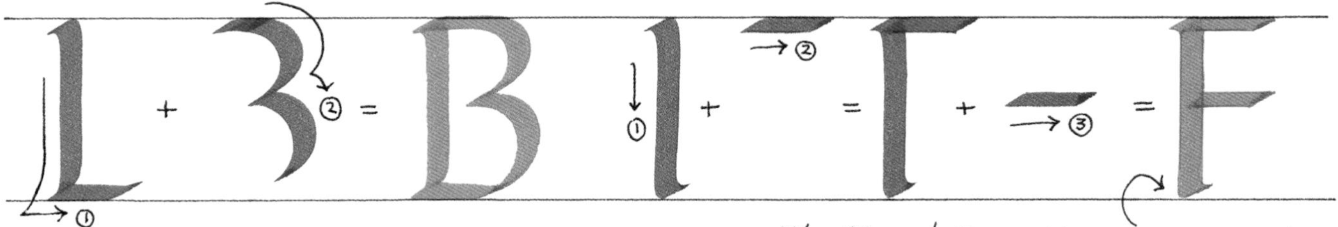

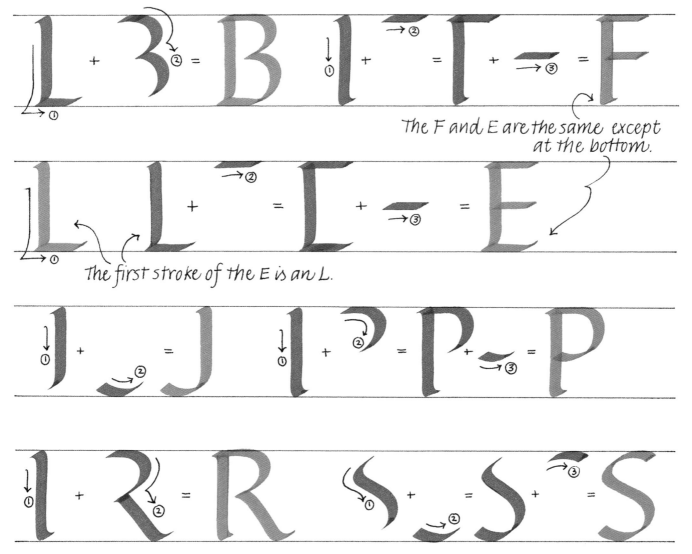

The F and E are the same except at the bottom.

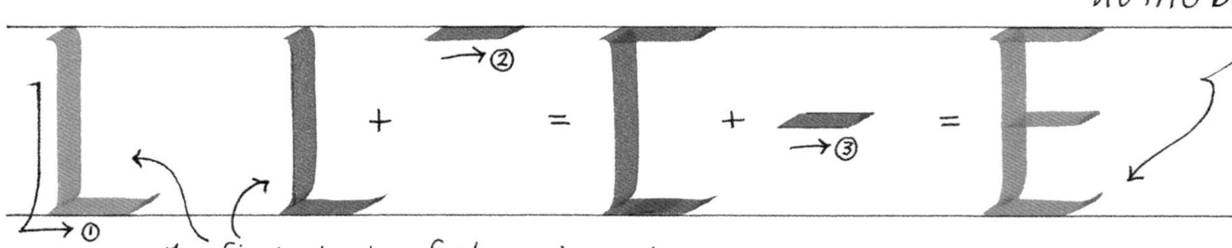

The first stroke of the E is an L.

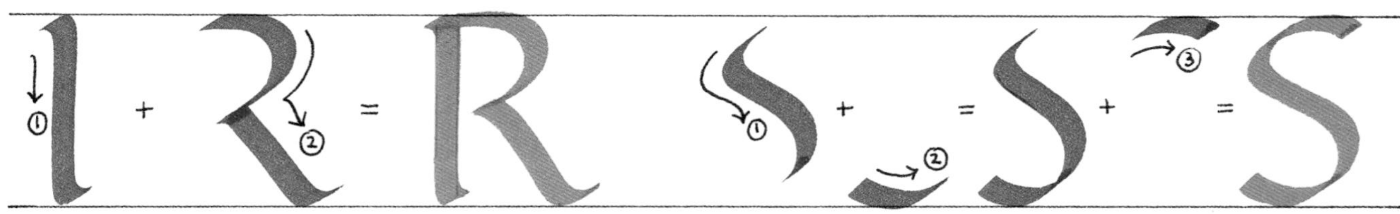

Start the S in the middle - not the top or bottom stroke.

THE EXTRA-WIDE LETTERS

The extra-wide letters are the **M** and **W.**

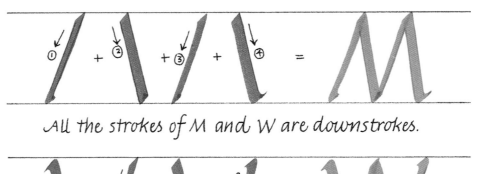

All the strokes of M and W are downstrokes.

SOMETHING EXTRA

Here's something you can try to make the **A, M, N, V, W, X,** and **Y** a little more graceful. When you make diagonal strokes from upper left to lower right, change your pen from the flattened pen position to the diagonal pen position (from 30° to 45°). The strokes will look like this.

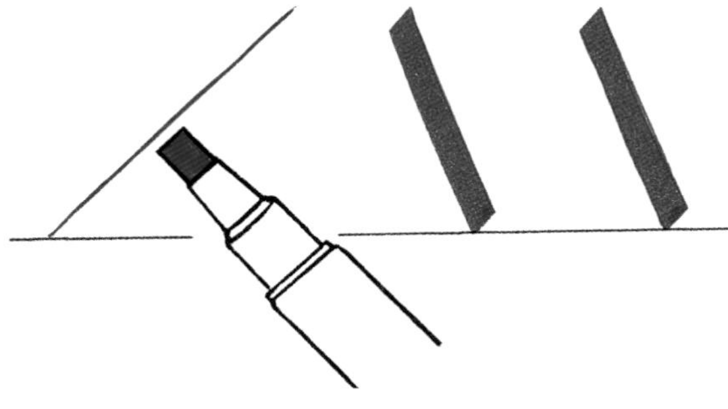

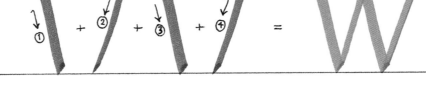

And the letters will look like this.

Try these letters first with your marker (**Roman #2** guide lines) and then with your fountain pen (with the **Roman #1** guide lines).

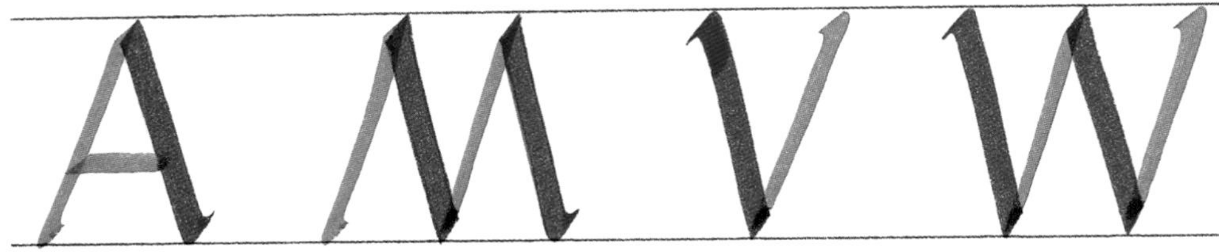

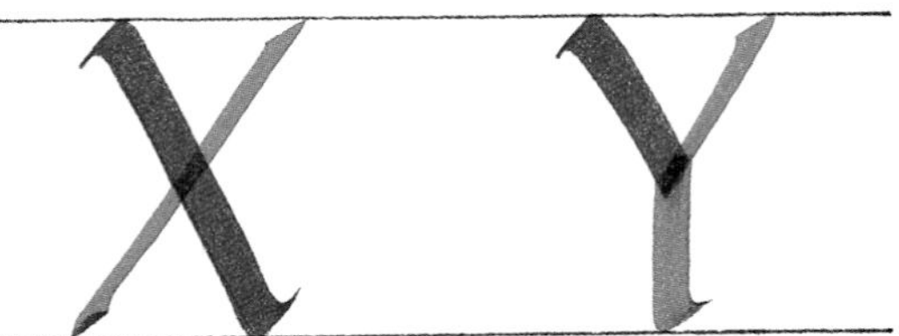

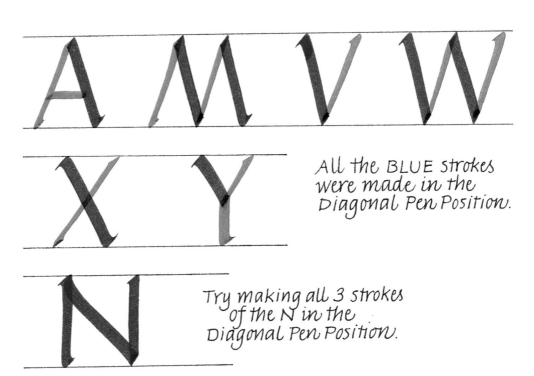

All the BLUE strokes were made in the Diagonal Pen Position.

Try making all 3 strokes of the N in the Diagonal Pen Position.

HOW TO PRACTICE

You can practice writing words using whichever pen you prefer—the chisel-edge calligraphy marker or the fountain pen—but be sure to use the correct guide lines. The words in the example below were written with a fountain pen.

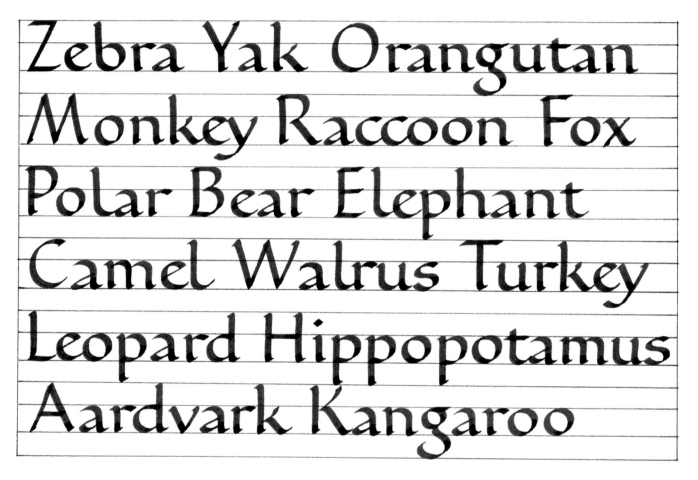

Zebra Yak Orangutan
Monkey Raccoon Fox
Polar Bear Elephant
Camel Walrus Turkey
Leopard Hippopotamus
Aardvark Kangaroo

Don't write too fast!

13

Numbers & Punctuation

NUMBERS

The good news about numbers is that there are only ten of them to learn. The bad news is that there isn't really a very interesting way to practice them besides simply writing them until you know them. It's not like learning letters, where you can practice by writing names, poetry, birthday cards, or copying lines from a favorite book. You could write your phone number a few times, but then what—?

But anyway, we all need to use numbers with our calligraphy once in a while, to write a date, an address, or maybe a time (such as on a party invitation). Here are the basic rules.

1. Numbers can be written in either pen position, the diagonal (45°) or the flattened (30°). It's a good idea to make the number using the same pen position as the alphabet you are currently writing. Use the diagonal pen position with Gothic and Italic, and use the flattened pen position with Roman and Uncial.

2. Make the numbers about the same height as the capitals or a little smaller. For Uncial, make them the height of the **l** or the **k** (the taller letters). You can be the judge of what looks right. If you make them too tall, they will look thin, and if they are too short, they will be too heavy.

3. If the alphabet you are using is slanted (Italic), slant the numbers in the same way. If the alphabet is vertical (Gothic, Uncial, Roman), make the numbers vertical as well.

Here are examples of numbers written with a fountain pen, in the diagonal pen position, first upright (vertical) and then slanted.

1 2 3 4 5 6 7 8 9 0

These numbers are SLANTED to go with Italic calligraphy:

1 2 3 4 5 6 7 8 9 0

This illustration shows the strokes for each of the numbers.

When writing numbers in groups, as opposed to one at a time, leave more space between them than you would for letters.

2 0 4 6 5

20465 Too close!

HOW TO PRACTICE

One way to practice your numbers is by writing some addresses. That way you can see how the numbers look in combination with letters.

Ms. Veronica Italic
563 East 42nd Street
Penland, NJ 07849

Mr. John Roman
7301 S. 46th Street
Alphabet City, GA
53896

PUNCTUATION

As soon as you start using your calligraphy for writing sentences or even greeting cards, you'll need to know punctuation. You will probably find this quite easy to learn, because a lot of punctuation marks are made like the dot on the Roman **i.**

You can hold your pen in either position for punctuation. Since it is normally part of writing, just keep your pen in the same position (pen angle) that you are using. That is, if you write a sentence in Italic or Gothic, your pen is already at the diagonal pen position.

In Uncial or Roman, you are at the flattened pen position.

Here are the **period, comma, colon, semicolon, quote marks,** and **apostrophe** in the diagonal pen position.

In fact, the two different pen positions don't make too much difference in the way these punctuation marks look.

The longer punctuation marks, the **exclamation point, question mark,** and **parentheses** are the same height as the capitals. For Uncial, make them the height of the taller letters.

The **ampersand** is a substitute for the word "and." It is one of the most decorative punctuation marks, and can be made a few different ways.

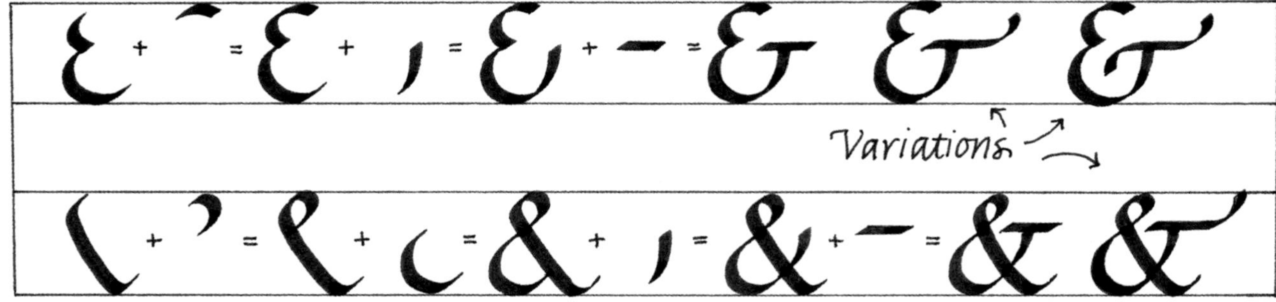

PART III

Using Your Calligraphy

14

Writing Smaller

Now that you have tried some of the alphabets in this book, you are ready to use your calligraphy in creative ways.

Of the four alphabets you have been working with, you probably have a favorite. You can use any alphabet in these projects or even a combination of alphabets. Just remember to try to make the letters the correct size for the pen you are using. If you are working with calligraphy markers, the letters will be bigger than those you make with the fountain pen.

SMALLER PEN NIB OR END

It's always nice to combine larger writing with smaller writing, in whichever hand (alphabet) you choose. If your calligraphy marker has two ends, you can now try writing with the smaller end (2 mm). Or if you are using markers with only one end, change to a 2-mm marker.

You may also find a smaller nib for your fountain pen labeled M or B-2. You can try writing your favorite alphabets using either the 2-mm marker or the small fountain-pen nib.

The guide lines for the 2-mm marker are the same as the ones for the larger (B or B-4) fountain pen. You'll see that they are labeled for use with "pointed marker, wide fountain pen (B or B-4), small calligraphy marker (2 mm)." Try writing your alphabets in the appropriate line spaces.

Here are the alphabets you've learned written smaller.

a b c d e f g h i j k l m

n o p q r s t u v w x y z

A B C D E F G H I

J K L M N O P Q

R S T U V W X Y Z

a b c d e f g h i j k l m

n o p q r s t u v w x y z

a b c d e f g h i j k l m
n o p q r s t u v w x y z

a b c d e f g h i j k l m n
o p q r s t u v w x y z

A B C D E F G H I
J K L M N O P Q R
S T U V W X Y Z

It is important to remember not to speed up. Sometimes when we write small, our tendency is to write quickly. Your calligraphy will always look better if you try to write slowly.

To use the smaller nib on the fountain pen, you'll have to unscrew the nib that's on the pen now (the B or B-4) and replace it with the smaller nib (the M or B-2). Be careful when you do this because you may get a bit inky. You can hold the old nib with a paper towel when you remove it from the pen. It's a good idea to rinse the nib with warm water to get the old ink off it before you put it away.

If you want to use colored ink (a colored cartridge) in your fountain pen, it's important to clean your pen, especially if you have been using black ink. Rinse out both the nib and the part of the pen that the nib screws into.

You can try your alphabets with the fountain pen, using the **Small Writing** guide lines for "small fountain pen (M or B-2)." There is no Gothic example here, because Gothic is usually too difficult to write so small.

This is an example of Italic written with the smaller fountain pen nib.

Also try writing other alphabets.

UNCIAL IS REALLY NICE WRITTEN SMALL, BUT NOT TOO FAST!

15

Border Designs

Calligraphy borders can be used to decorate stationery or greeting cards. They can also add something special to a page on which you write a text or a poem. You can make border designs out of strokes, like zigzags or crosses, or by using letters or parts of letters.

Here are examples of borders made of calligraphic strokes or parts of letters.

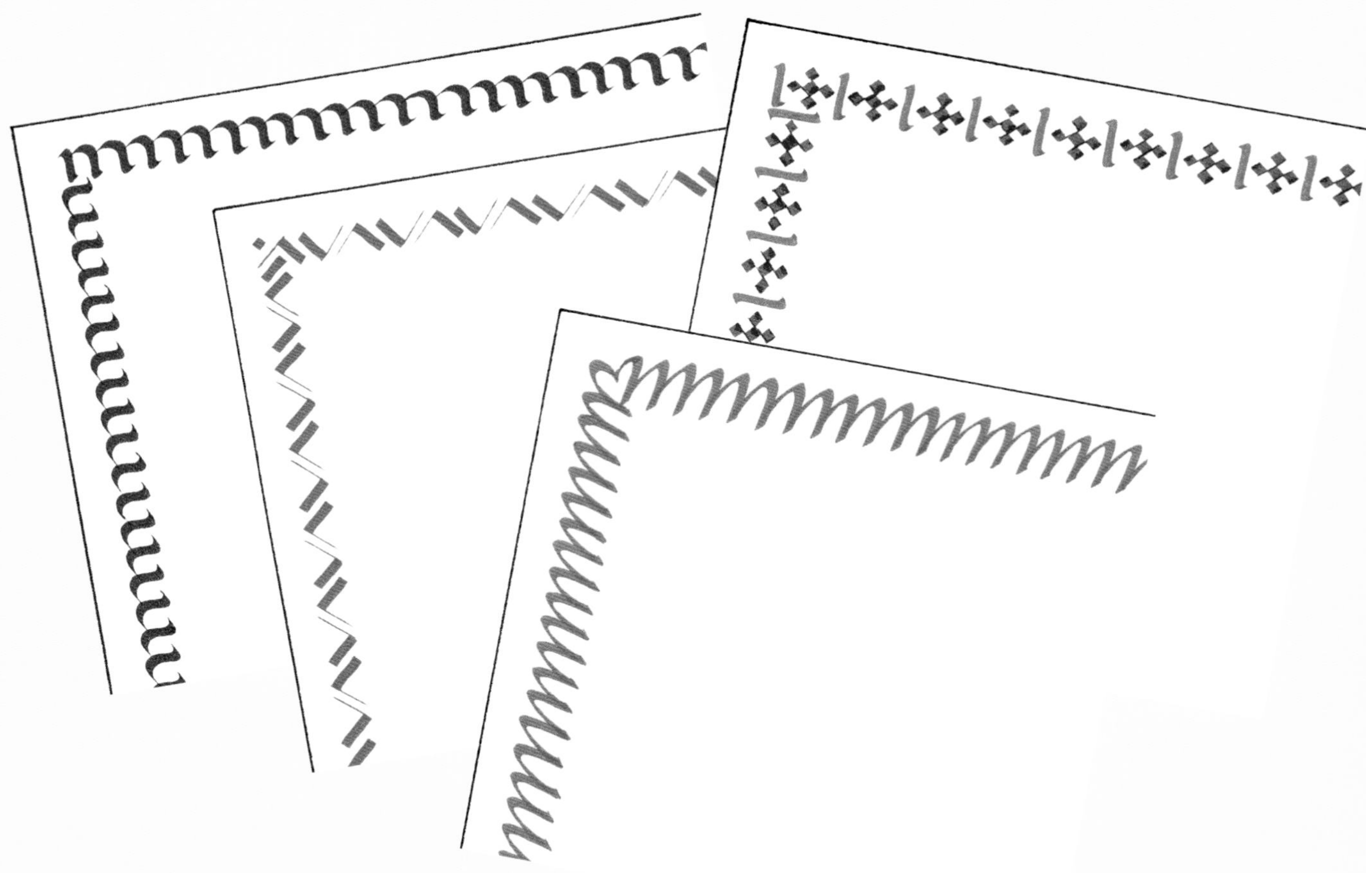

An alphabet border can be made of one letter repeated, a series of letters (such as your initials), or a repeated word or phrase, like "Happy Birthday" or "Thank You."

In order to position the border on your paper, you'll need to draw some lines. First make an outline around the edge of the paper, using a pencil. Decide how far the border should be from the paper's edge. If you want it ½ inch (1.25 cm) or 1 inch (2.5 cm) from the edge, measure your lines carefully from each side of the paper. Don't press too hard on your pencil or the lines will be hard to erase.

This pencil line will be the bottom (baseline) of the border.

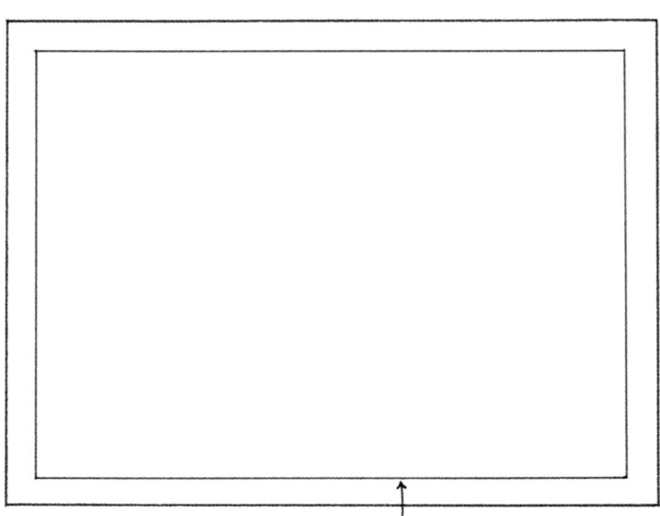

Draw this line in pencil.

Next, draw another line for the top of the border. You can also make this line as close or as far away as you like, within reasonable limits. If you are making a letter border, the top line should be the correct distance down from the top of the letter. If you are using lowercase letters, the waistline is all you need (the top of the x-height, or smaller lowercase letters).

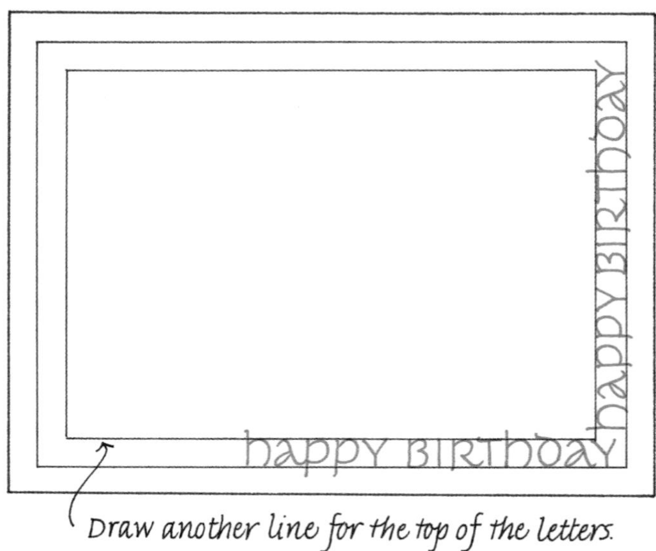

Draw another line for the top of the letters.

If your border design is made of calligraphic strokes, but not letters, you can try different measurements for your top line, like this.

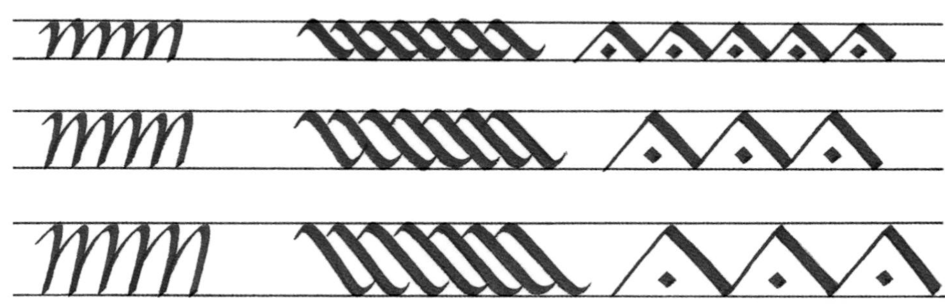

These designs were all made with the same pen, but the spaces between the lines are different.

You can make borders with your markers, using two or three colors, or even both ends of the marker, so that part of the design is bigger and part smaller, like this.

You could make a nice gift with a border of someone's name or initials printed on stationery. This can be printed inexpensively at many copy shops. Make the border on a piece of white 8½ × 11-inch (21.5 × 28-cm) practice paper, writing in black ink with your fountain pen. The reason you should use black is that it will reproduce better than colored ink or colored marker.

Actually, it is also possible to make your design in color and have colored copies made in a photocopy shop, but it is usually much more expensive.

Then take the paper to a copy shop where you can have photocopies made on many different kinds of paper. Many copy shops will offer you a choice of papers of different colors or textures. (You may have to ask them what they have besides ordinary white paper.)

If you like, you can get a multicolored package of paper and have your stationery printed on all different colors. This makes a great gift, especially with a package of envelopes that either match or contrast with the papers you've selected.

ERASING THE LINES

When you draw your own guide lines in pencil, you have a choice: to erase or not to erase. If you don't press too hard on your pencil and your lines are light enough, it's OK to leave them. If you prefer to erase the lines, here are a few rules to follow.

1. Wait until the ink is *really* dry before erasing lines.

2. Use a good eraser, such as a kneaded eraser or a plastic eraser, available in an art-supply shop. They are cheap and work much better than the eraser at the end of your pencil.

3. When erasing the lines, try to erase above and below your calligraphy, rather than rubbing directly over it, so that your letters don't smear.

16

Greeting Cards

Handmade greeting cards are fun to make and a real pleasure to receive.

You can use your calligraphy to make cards from scratch or to decorate cards that are already printed. Buy packages of blank cards with envelopes at stationery or art supply stores, or cut and fold paper to make your own cards.

If you use heavy paper, you probably won't be able to see the printed guide lines through the paper, so you will need to draw some lines yourself.

It's also fun to make cards using colored paper, but always be sure that the paper won't absorb the ink. This is less likely to happen when you write with your calligraphy markers or other felt-tip pens, but fountain-pen ink is sometimes absorbed by the paper, or "bleeds." It's a good idea to test your pen or marker on a scrap of the paper that you plan to make the card from. You want to be sure that the ink and the paper work well together. If the paper bleeds, try using different paper.

SIMPLE FOLDED CARDS

There are lots of ways that you can make a simple folded card look lively and attractive. One way is by writing your message large with a colored calligraphy marker and putting a border around it, using the smaller end of the marker or your fountain pen. Here are some steps to do this.

1. Choose the card size that you want to use, for example 5 × 7 inches (12.5 × 17.5 cm), shown in the example on the next page. You can hold the card either vertically or horizontally.

2. Draw an outline of your card on a piece of practice paper. You can use this outline to help decide how you want the words to be positioned on the finished card.

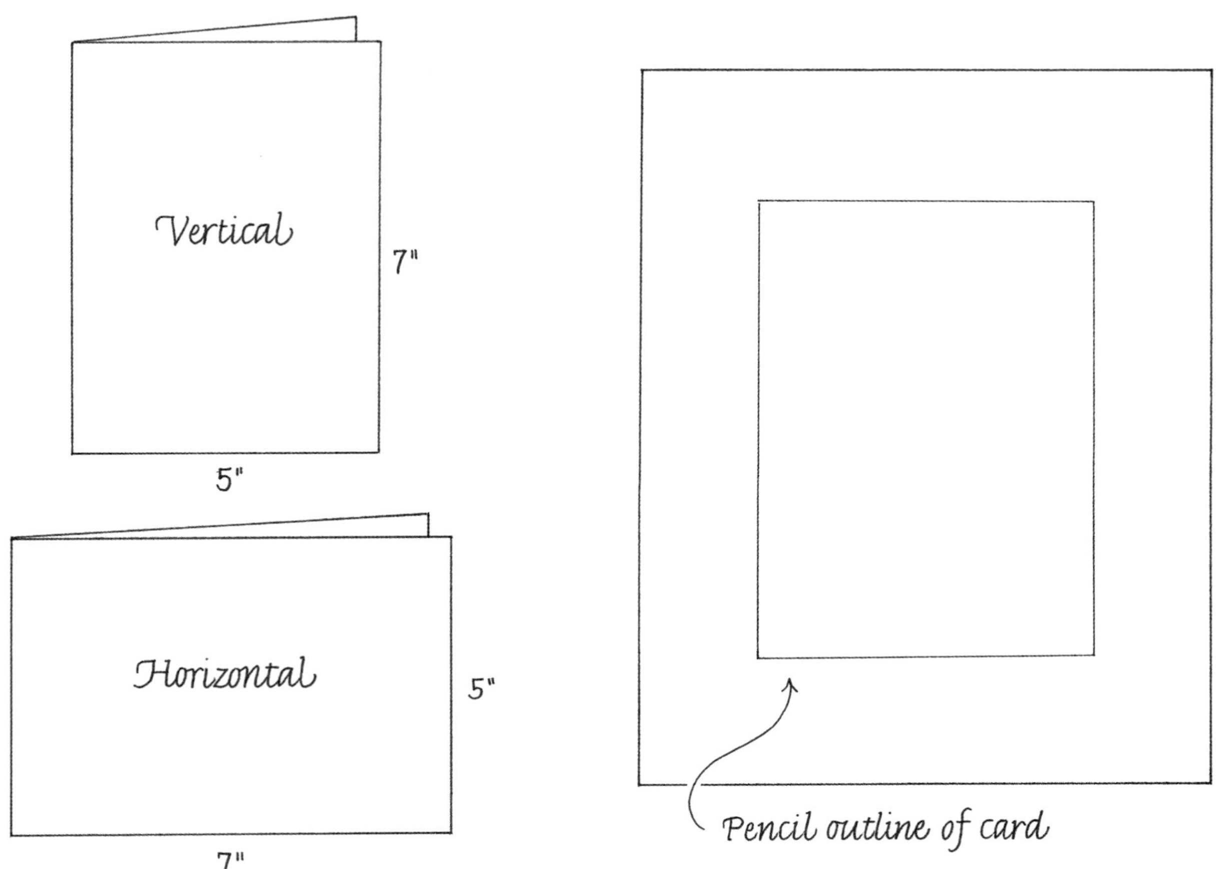

3. Write your message on another piece of practice paper, using the correct guide lines for the pen or marker and the alphabet that you choose. Try writing the message several different ways.

Happy Birthday

Happy
Birthday

Happy Birthday

Happy
Birthday

happy
BIRTHDAY

■ **4.** Cut out the messages and lay them on the outline drawing of your card to find a good position for the words. This is how you can figure out the **layout.** Try it a few different ways until you find one layout that you like.

Happy Birthday

Let's use this layout

■ **5.** Draw pencil lines on your card, putting the lines in the same position as they are in your layout. Drawing the lines is the hard part. If you can see through your card, you can use your printed guide lines. If not, you will need to start by making a baseline for your words. Then you can either draw the top line for the x-height of the lowercase letters (also called the waistline) or draw the line for the top of the capitals, if you are writing in all capitals. Use a ruler and try not to make the lines too dark.

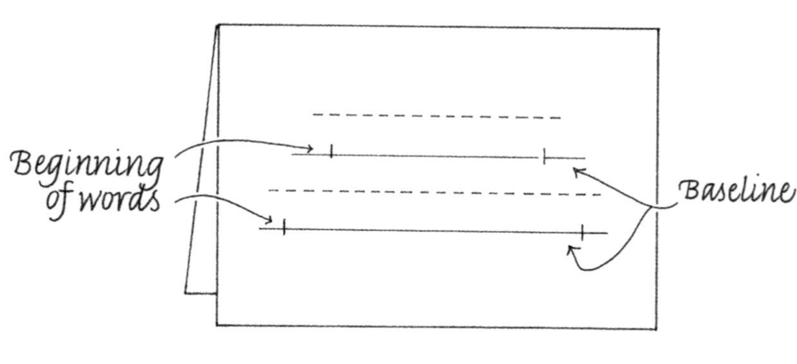

Another way to draw the guide lines: Just draw the baseline for each line of writing on the card. Then try estimating the height of the letters. You may be surprised at how good your calligraphy is with only a baseline.

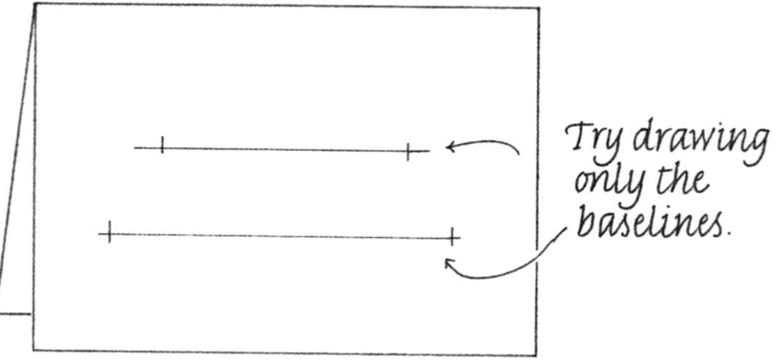

■ **6.** Write the words directly on the card, using the pencil lines and your layout as a guide.

■ **7.** After you put your message on the card, you can make a border around it (see Chapter 15, "Border Designs") or just put a "calligraphic ornament" in each corner of the card, like this.

These are "calligraphic ornaments"

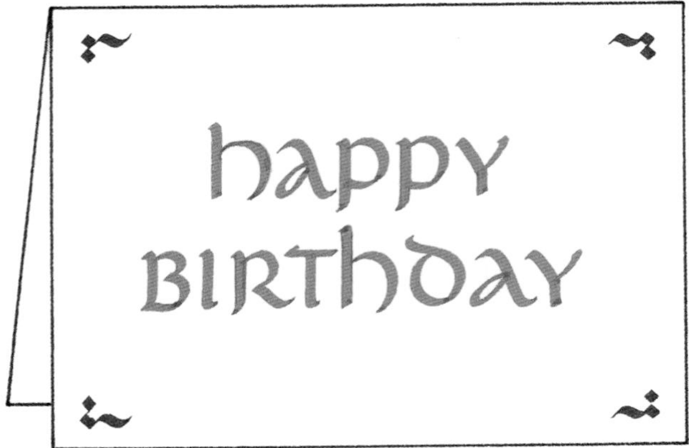

■ **8.** You can also decorate your card by using a different colored marker and making little diamond shapes here and there on the card. Or you can make a free-form border by making a squiggly line all around the card.

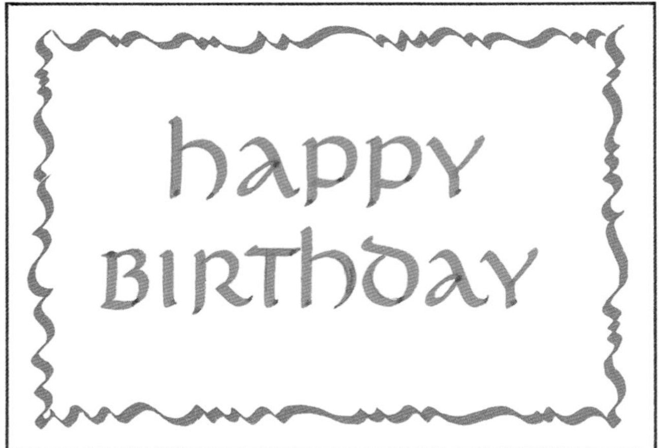

9. Use metallic markers or gel pens to decorate your letters, if you wish. Here are some possibilities.

10. On the inside of the card, you can write whatever you like using your calligraphy markers or fountain pens. It's a good idea to write smaller on the inside, which means using the smaller fountain-pen nib or the small end of the marker.

11. You could write the name of the person you're giving the card to on the outside and the message on the inside, with or without decoration.

To Mom,
With love,
Michael

Inside message

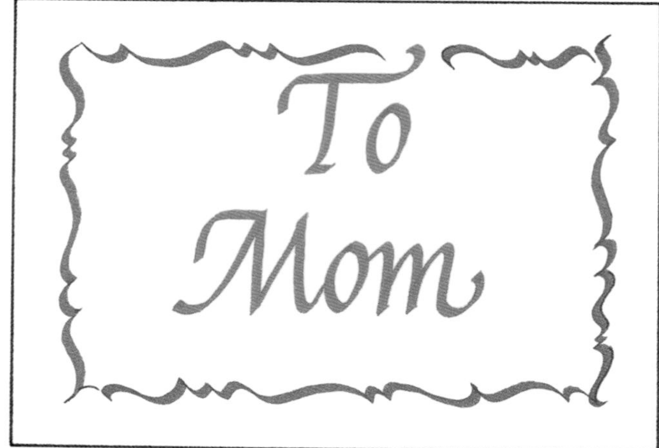

Books on handmade greeting cards show you how to make pop-up cards and special folded cards in all kinds of shapes and forms. Making these cards is great fun and gives you the opportunity to use your calligraphy on one-of-a-kind cards. We'll show you just one special card that's very easy to make. It's called an accordion-fold card.

ACCORDION-FOLD CARDS

To make this card, you'll need a long strip of paper. You can try the measurements below or make one that's smaller or bigger. Here are the steps.

1. Cut out a strip of paper that measures 2 × 16 inches (5 × 40 cm) using paper that is a little heavier than your practice paper. Fold it in half. (The broken lines in these drawings show where to fold the paper.)

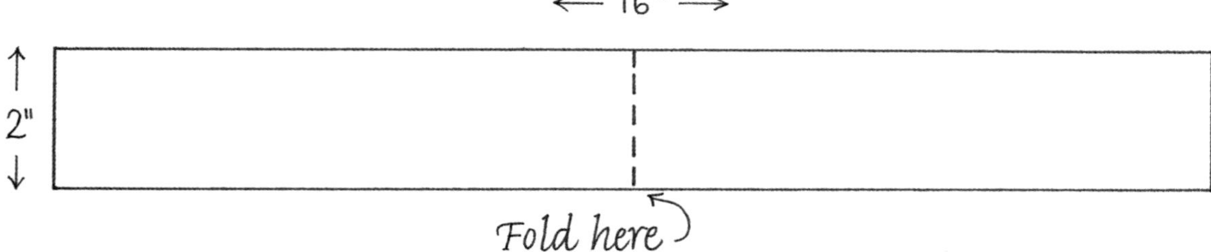

2. Fold each half in half again, folding it backwards to the center crease.

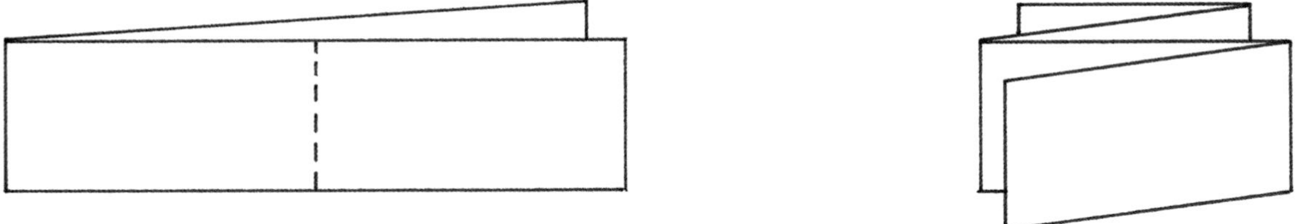

3. Fold each section backwards once again toward the creases so that the strip makes a zigzag.

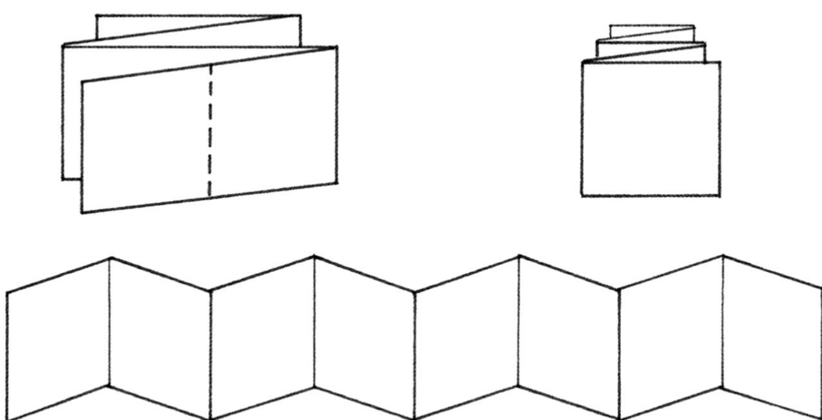

■ **4.** When you press it flat, it should look like a little square book.

■ **5.** You now have eight squares to write in. You can divide your message into seven or eight parts, like this.

Do this step in pencil or with your pointed marker on a piece of practice paper. That way you can figure out how the words can be divided before you write on the actual card.

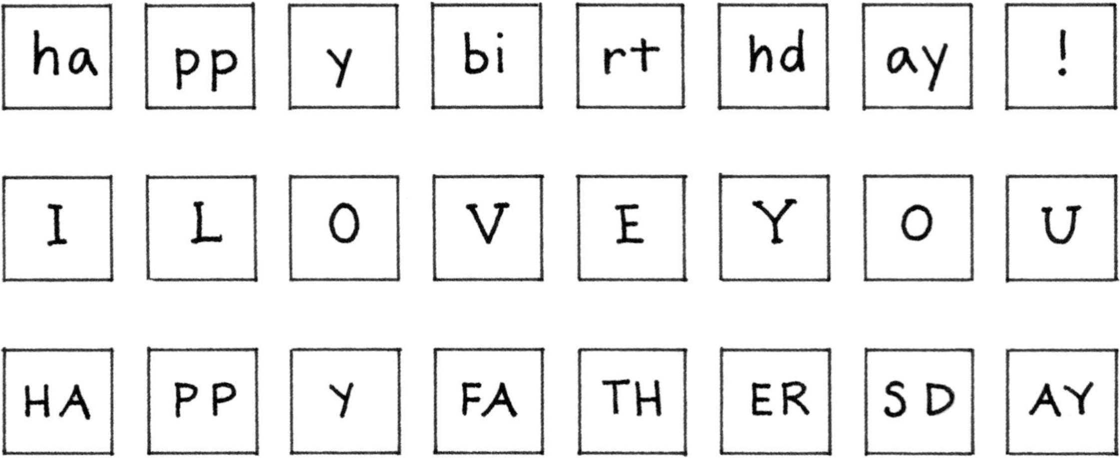

■ **6.** Using your calligraphy marker, write one or two letters in each square. If you like, you can use a different color for each word or each letter or each square. Try to write without your guide lines; it's easier than you think, when the space is small and the marker is big!

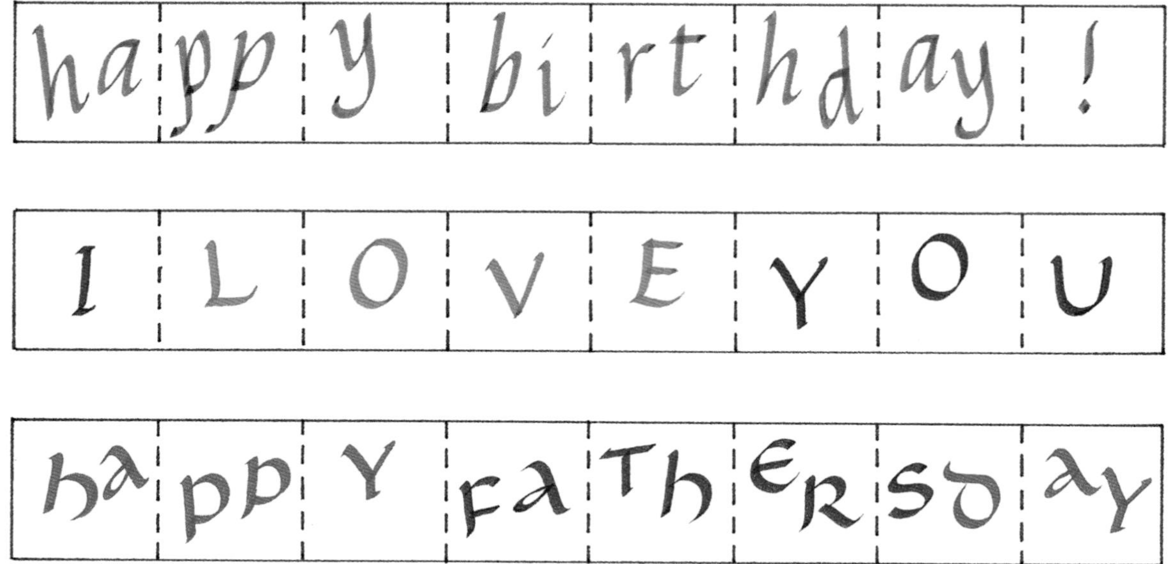

■ **7.** You can decorate the "cover" of the card (the back of square #1) any way you like, perhaps with the name of the recipient ("To Dad," "Mary Ann," or whatever). Or you could use a drawing or a photo. It's fun to cut out a photo of the person who is receiving the card and glue it onto the cover.

■ **8.** If you tie a ribbon around the accordion card, it becomes a card and a book in one. If you glue the ribbon to the back of the card, it won't fall off.

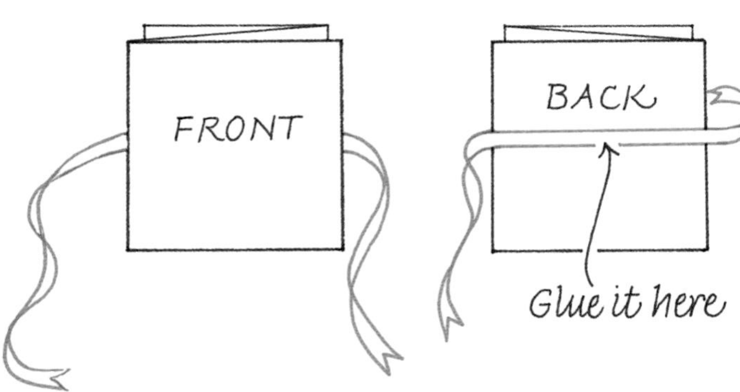

You can also make a bigger accordion-fold card with four parts instead of eight. Use it to write a longer message, or even to combine calligraphy with drawings, photos, or whatever you like. Try using a strip of paper measuring 3 × 12 inches (7.5 × 30 cm) or 4 × 16 inches (10 × 40 cm) for a four-part card, and fold it twice rather than four times.

If you want to glue something into the accordion card, be sure that the paper you use is fairly thick.

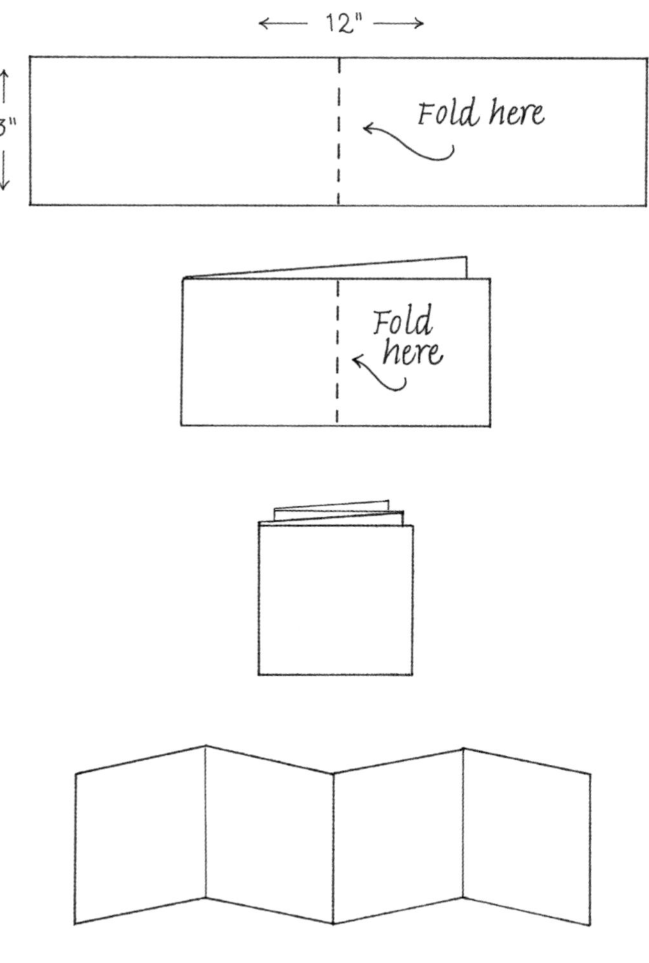

Hot Tip! If you are making one-of-a-kind cards, always try your cards on practice paper before working on "good" paper. Mostly when we make something in calligraphy, we need to try it a couple of times to be sure that the layout is right and the letters look the way we want them to. If you make a few examples on your practice paper, you can see what looks best before starting on the finished card.

Another Tip! Have extra blank cards on hand so that you can do it over if you aren't satisfied or if you make a spelling mistake. We all make lots of mistakes, even after years of experience!

COPY-MACHINE GREETING CARDS

Another possibility for calligraphic greeting cards is to make one original and have it printed on a photocopier (copy machine). The easiest way is to do the calligraphy on white paper in black ink or with a black marker, and then have it copied on white or colored paper. The letters will come out in black but you can decorate the card with colored markers or in many other ways.

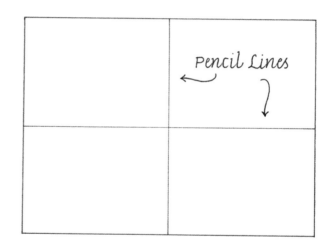

Here's one way to prepare your cards.

1. Using an 8½ × 11-inch (21 × 27.5-cm) piece of paper (standard photocopier size), draw a pencil line (pressing lightly on the pencil) through the center of the paper in each direction, like this.

Pencil Lines

You can also fold the paper twice, instead of drawing the lines. Either way, the paper will be divided into four parts.

■ **2.** Write your calligraphy message in the lower half of the page if you are holding the paper horizontally, or in the boxes on the right half of the page if you are holding it vertically. Use one section of the paper for each message. You can either write the same message twice or write two different messages.

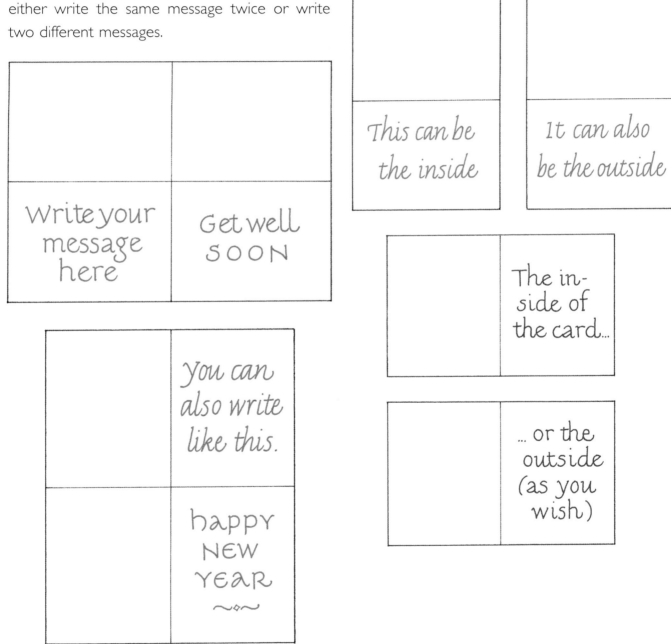

Write your message here

Get well SOON

You can also write like this.

happy NEW YEAR

■ **3.** Bring this page to a copy shop and have copies made on whatever paper you like (white, colored, textured, thin, thick). Then cut the copies along the shorter center line, as shown.

This can be the inside

It can also be the outside

The in-side of the card...

... or the outside (as you wish)

■ **4.** Fold your cards with the message either on the inside or the outside. See right.

■ **5.** You can decorate or write on the other part of the card, as you like. Easy?

Hot Tip! If you are having something printed, you can make corrections (before it's printed), using white correction fluid. You can't write over the whited-out places, but you can use correction fluid to cover any blots or spots on the card or if you started writing in the wrong place. The white corrections won't show at all after the copies are made.

Another possibility is to make a double-fold card, with calligraphy on the inside and the outside with a two-part message. Here's how to do this.

■ **1.** Take a piece of 8½ × 11-inch (21 × 27.5-cm) paper and fold it in half and in half again.

The top and left sides of the card will have the folds, and the bottom and right side will be open.

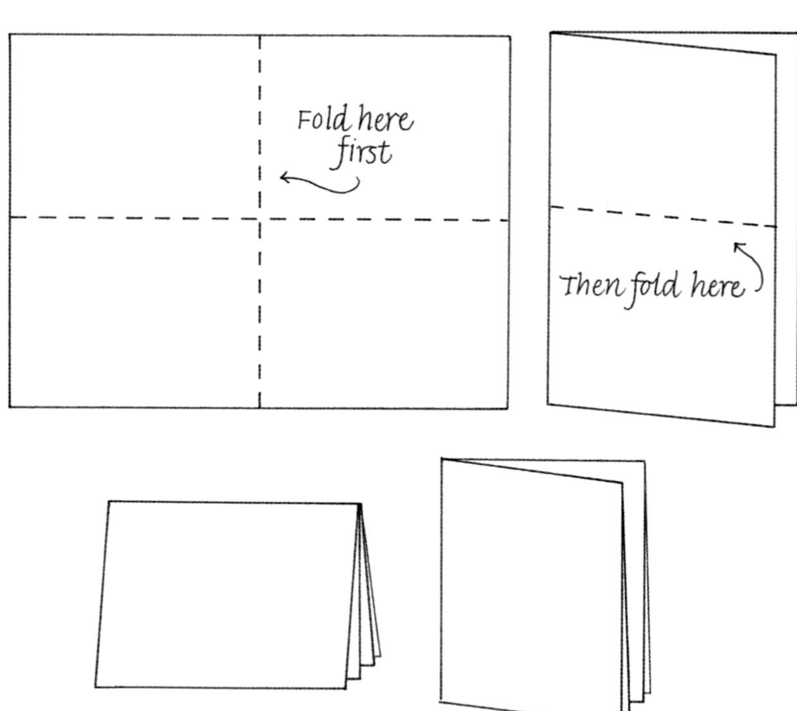

2. Then open the card and lay it flat. Write the first part of your message in the bottom right-hand section of the paper. You can hold it horizontally or vertically.

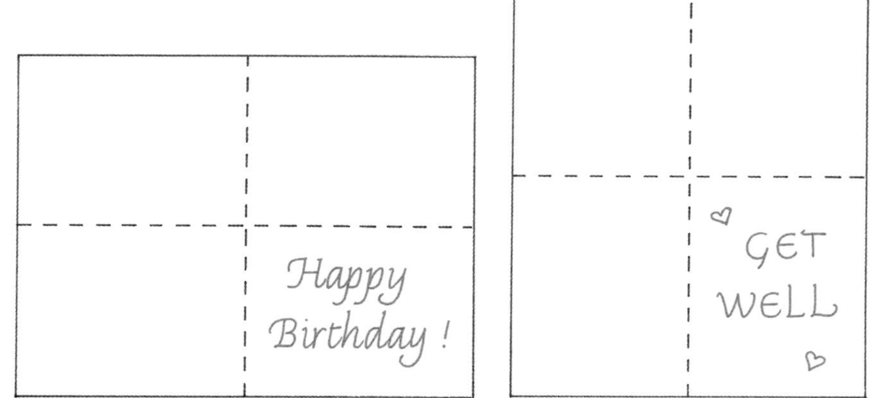

3. Then turn the paper upside down and write the second part of the message in the same section of the paper. It will look like this.

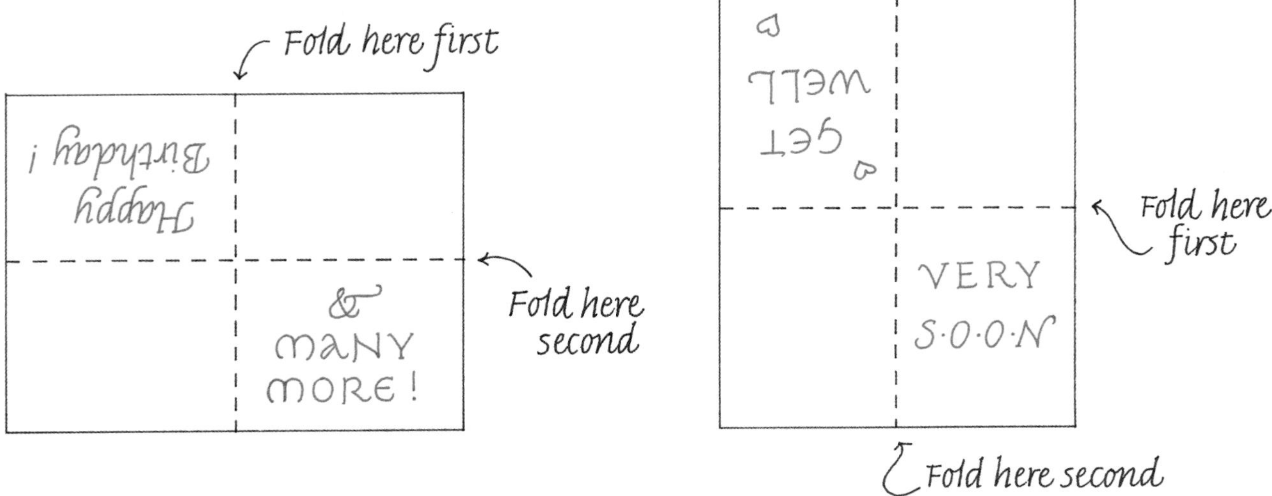

4. After you have copies made, fold the papers in the same way as you folded them in step 1. The messages will appear on the outside and the inside of the cards.

17

Party Invitations

It's especially nice to receive a handmade invitation. It's also fun to make one for your next party. In this chapter, we'll make a simple birthday party invitation that you can print on a photocopier.

This invitation is made the same way as a copy-machine greeting card (see Chapter 18), with writing on the outside and the inside. Here are the steps to follow.

1. Take an 8½ × 11-inch (21 × 27.5-cm) piece of plain white paper and draw lines (lightly) to divide it into quarters. You can also do this by folding it twice.

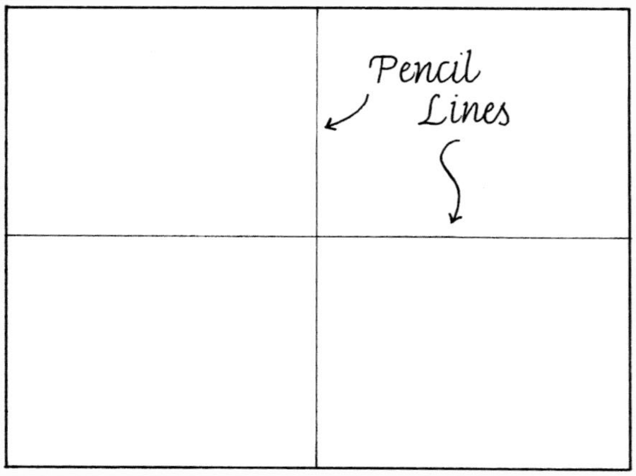

2. The calligraphy will go in the lower right and upper left boxes, so that when you fold the invitation, the writing will all face in the same direction.

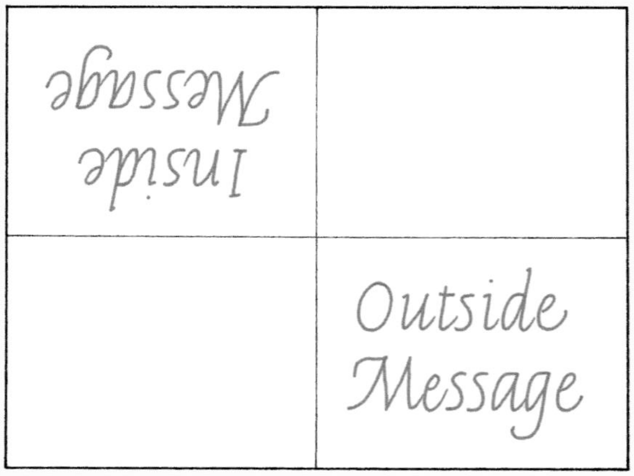

3. Decide what words you want on the outside of the invitation, for example, "It's a Party," or "You're Invited," or "A Birthday Party!" Write the words a couple times on practice paper, using the calligraphy you prefer, trying it a few different ways until you find one you like. Be sure the space on the practice paper is the same size as the box you will write in on the invitation.

You're Invited

You're Invited

You're Invited

YOU'RE INVITED

4. Do the calligraphy, using your guide lines, in the lower right quarter of the 8½ × 11-inch (21 × 27.5-cm) paper. Use black ink or a black marker. You won't have to draw your own guide lines because you will be able to see through the paper.

You may have to do this part a few times until you are satisfied with the way it looks.

You're Invited

5. The other part (the inside) of the invitation can be very simple. One possibility is drawing straight lines (with a fine-point black marker and a ruler) and then writing the words **For, Date, Time,** and **Place** at the beginning of each line. These words will have to be written small, using either the smaller fountain-pen nib, or a pointed marker, so that they don't take up too much space.

Leave an extra line at the bottom for the address. Don't forget to turn the paper around so that the outside and inside messages are facing in opposite directions.

You're Invited

For__________
Date__________
Time__________
Place__________
____

6. After you have the cards printed, you can fill in all the information using your colored markers or fountain pens. That way you can use the cards for your next party.

For Sarah's Birthday
Date March 9th
Time 2:00 pm
Place 35 Second Ave.
Brooklyn, NY

7. Or, if you wish, you can write all the information out before you have the invitation printed. This saves time, but may not be quite as much fun. If you are inviting a lot of people, this may be the best solution.

A Birthday Party
March 9, 2:00 pm
35 Second Ave.
Brooklyn
~ Sarah T. ~

8. You can also add your guests' names in calligraphy after the invitations are printed. If you plan to do this, be sure to leave some space on the invitation.

Leave space here

You're
Invited

To Danny ~
You're
Invited

Hot Tip! If you do the calligraphy on the front of the invitation on an angle (running uphill), or with the letters going up and down (see below), your writing can be a little uneven and no one will notice.

Another Tip! You can decorate your invitations after they are printed to make them more colorful, using colored markers, metallic markers, gel pens, or stickers. There are lots of birthday or party stickers available with pictures of balloons, ribbons, cakes, or gifts that you can put on your invitations. If you make your invitations in a copy shop, the calligraphy will probably be in black; decorating the invitations will add color and make them sparkle.

One More Tip! Don't forget that you can have your invitations copied on colored paper.

What's Next?

WHERE TO FROM HERE?

Learning calligraphy opens far more doors than we ever imagined. Once you have studied one or two different alphabets, you will want to learn new ones. Yes, there are many more styles of calligraphy besides the four in this book! Once you have worked with a couple different sizes of pens, you'll want to write bigger or smaller or both.

Markers are a good beginning and fountain pens are fine, but there are also dip-pens and brushes. You can also learn to write with a quill (a goose or turkey feather, made into a pen), and to make your own quills.

And there's a whole world of color to learn about, as well as all kinds of wonderful papers that you can write on or make things from.

Try writing on papers with different colors and textures to see what looks and feels good. There is no right or wrong about art materials, although some tools and materials are easier to work with or better suited to calligraphy. When you try different materials you'll get all kinds of ideas.

How do we learn all these things? There are lots of possibilities. Go to the library or a bookstore and look at the calligraphy books. Look at the materials in art-supply stores; some have pen or paper departments. Look for the calligraphy mail-order shops that advertise on the Internet. They are happy to send you a free catalog full of information and products that you'll find interesting—"how-to" books, calligraphy history books, or craft books showing you lots of projects to do with your calligraphy. The catalogs also show you many kinds of art supplies that calligraphers use, with information about the different materials (how they work, what they are good for). Some books and materials are expensive, but many things won't cost much.

Perhaps you can find a calligraphy class that you can join on weekends or after school. Some classes welcome kids; some do not, but it's always worth asking. If you can get a few friends interested, your school might organize a class for you.

It's also fun to start a calligraphy club where you can practice with your friends and work on projects together. You won't need any special facilities for this, just a table where you can sit together and share your ideas and maybe your art supplies as well. Having other people to practice with can make calligraphy more fun; plus you can learn from each other. You may be able to find someone in your area to teach a group of kids something special—a new alphabet, a different way to make handmade cards, or other kinds of arts and crafts that include calligraphy.

You are now a member of a very special group of people who love letters and the wonderful world they open for us.

GUIDE LINES

Pen Positions

Diagonal Pen Position

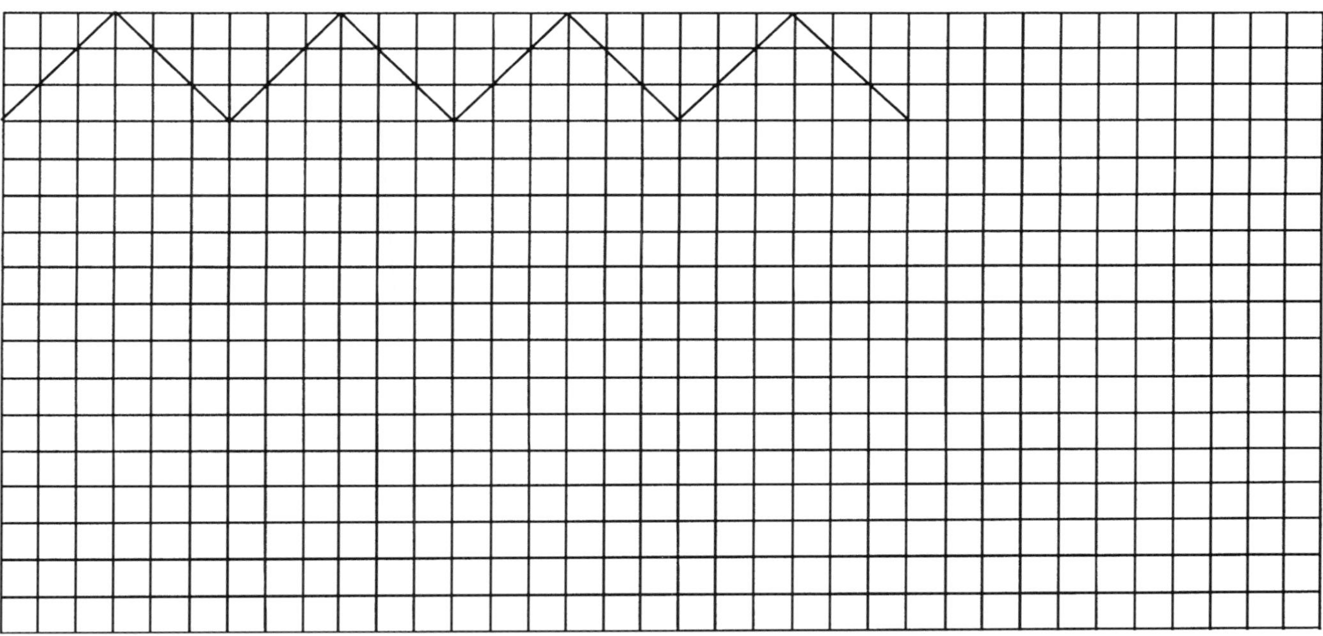

Flattened Pen Position

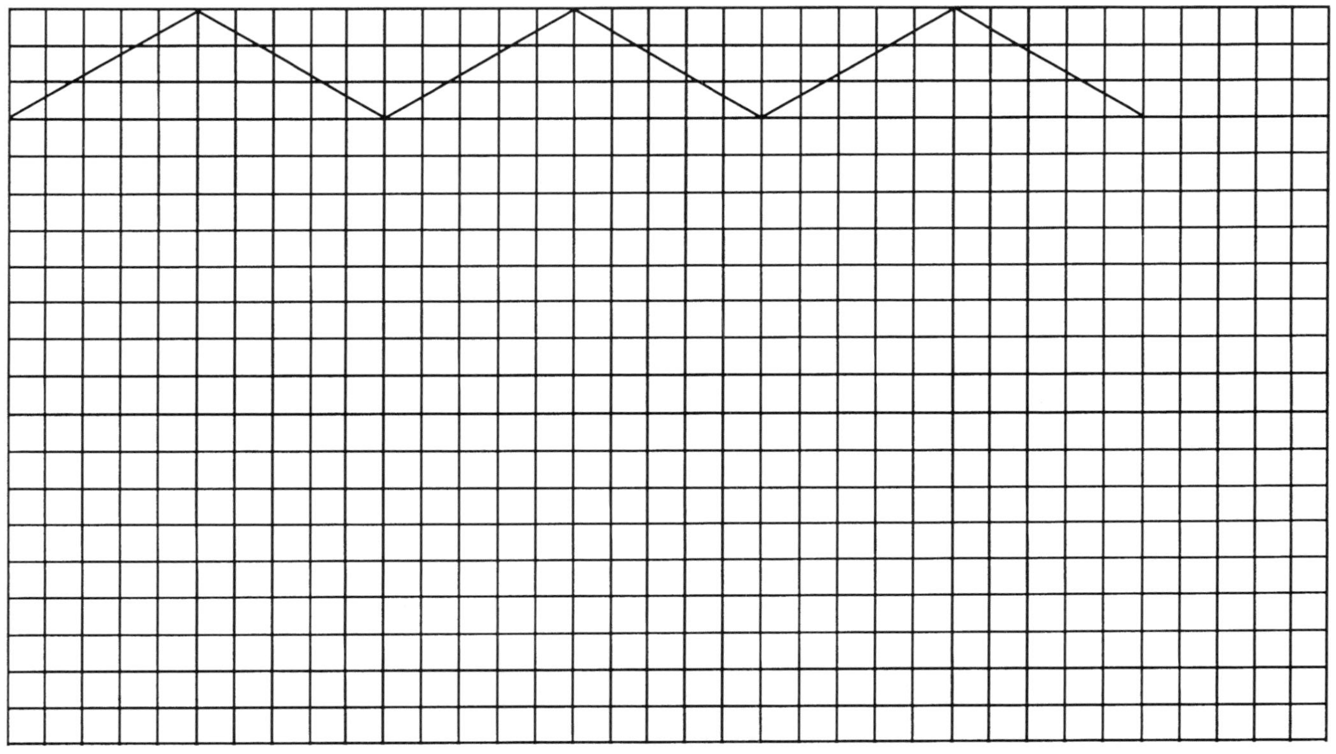

Italic #1

Pointed Marker, Wide Fountain Pen (B or B-4) Small Calligraphy Marker (2 mm)

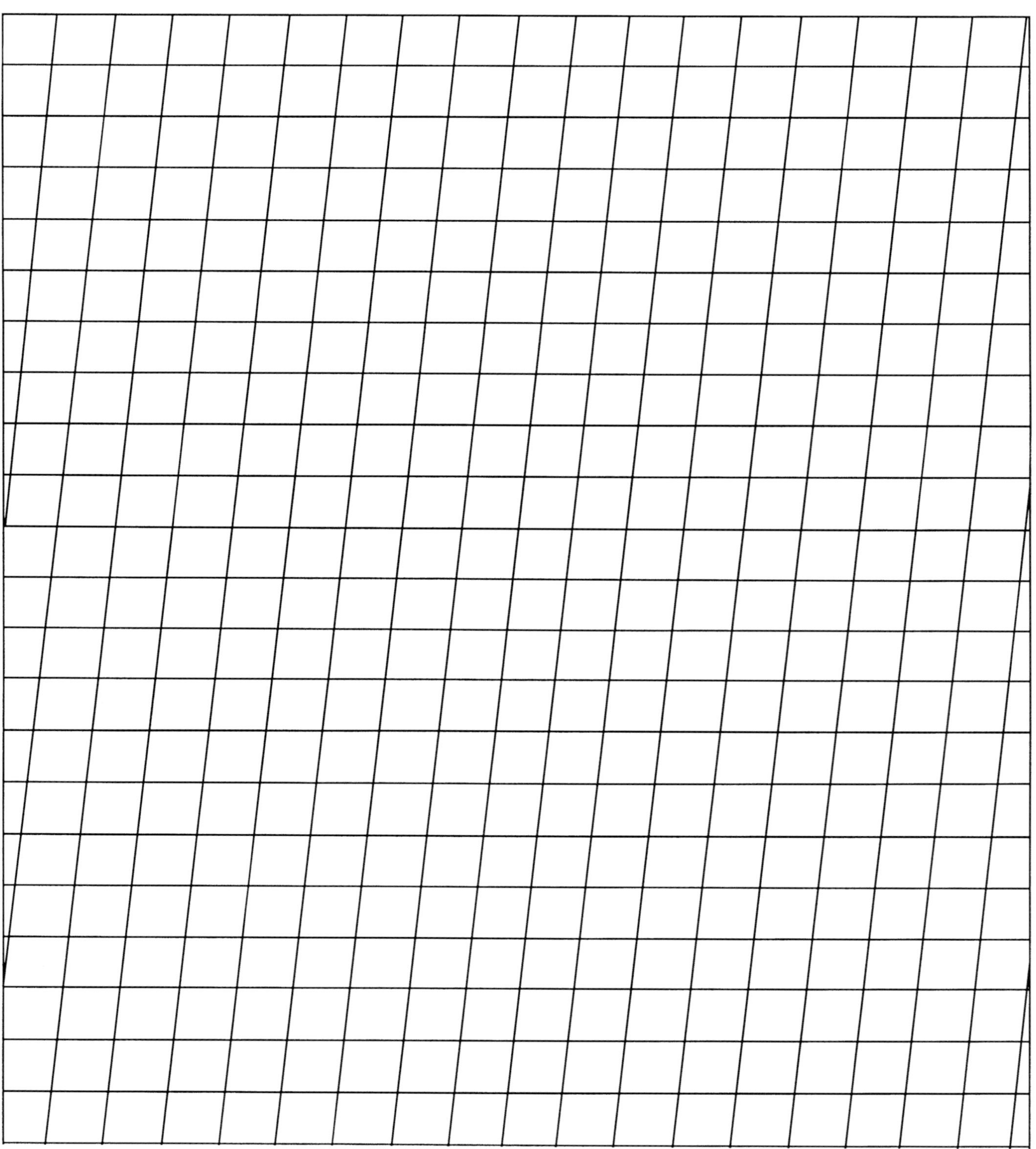

Italic #2

Wide Calligraphy Marker (3.5 mm)

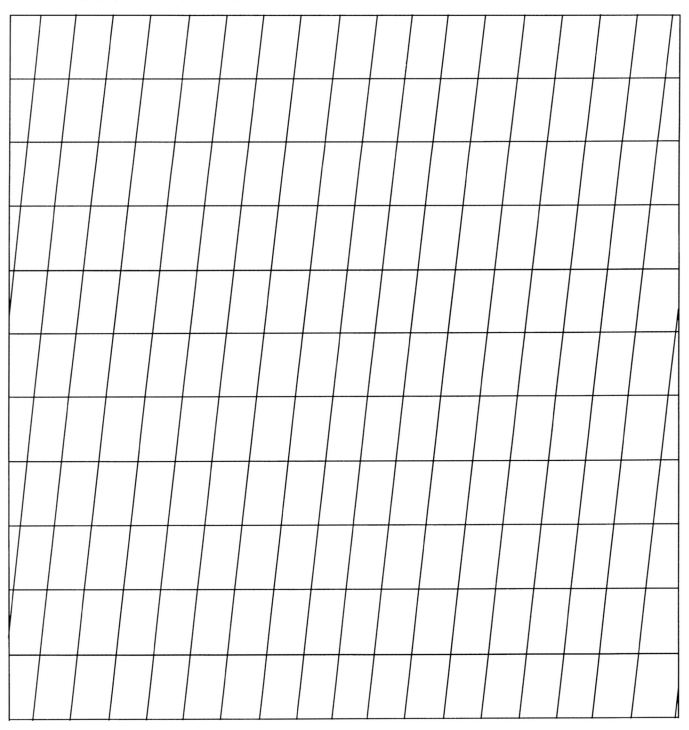

Gothic #1

Wide Calligraphy Marker (3.5 mm)

Gothic #2

Wide Fountain Pen (B or B-4), Small Calligraphy Marker (2 mm)

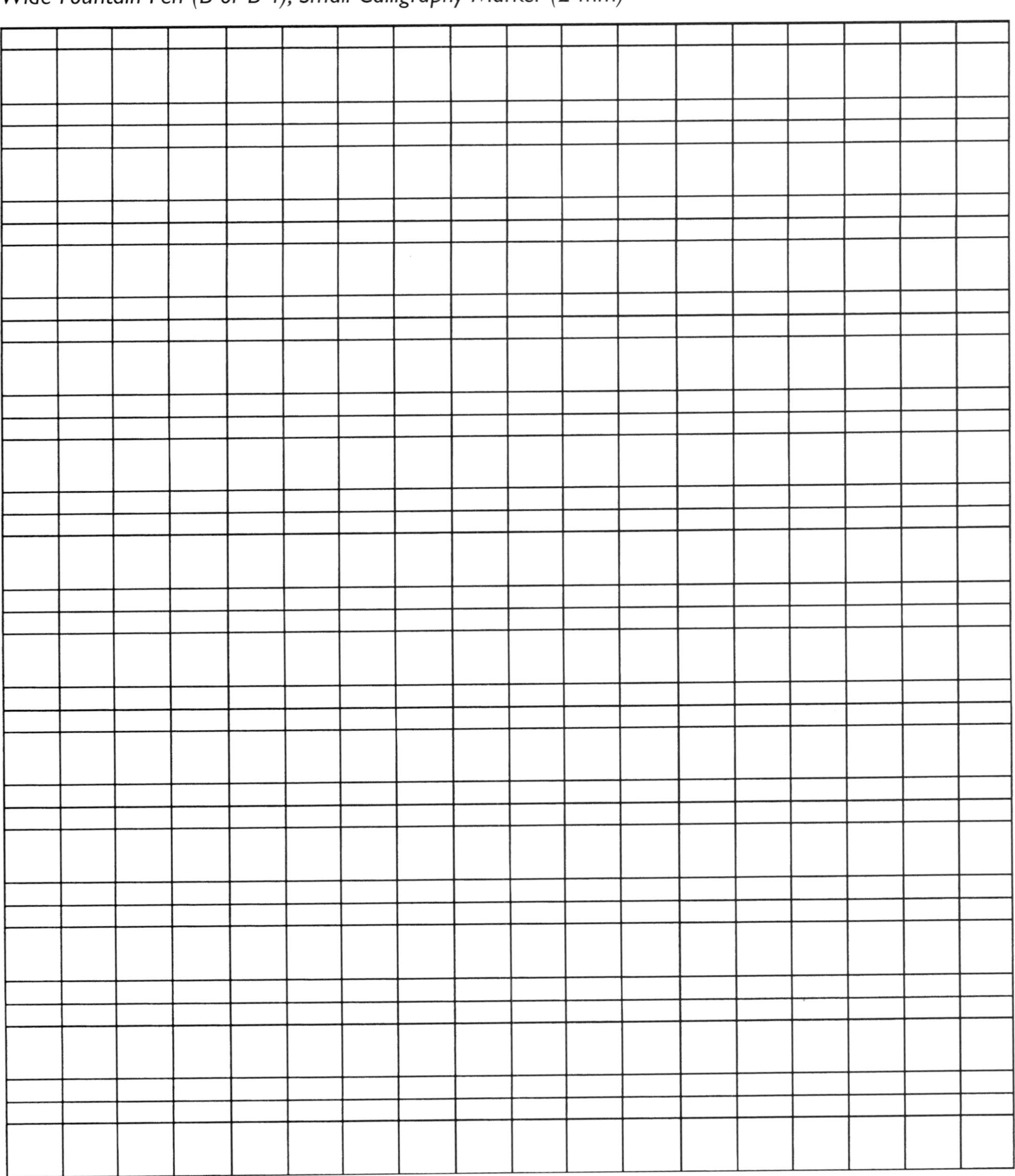

Uncial #1

Pointed Marker, Wide Calligraphy Marker (3.5 mm)

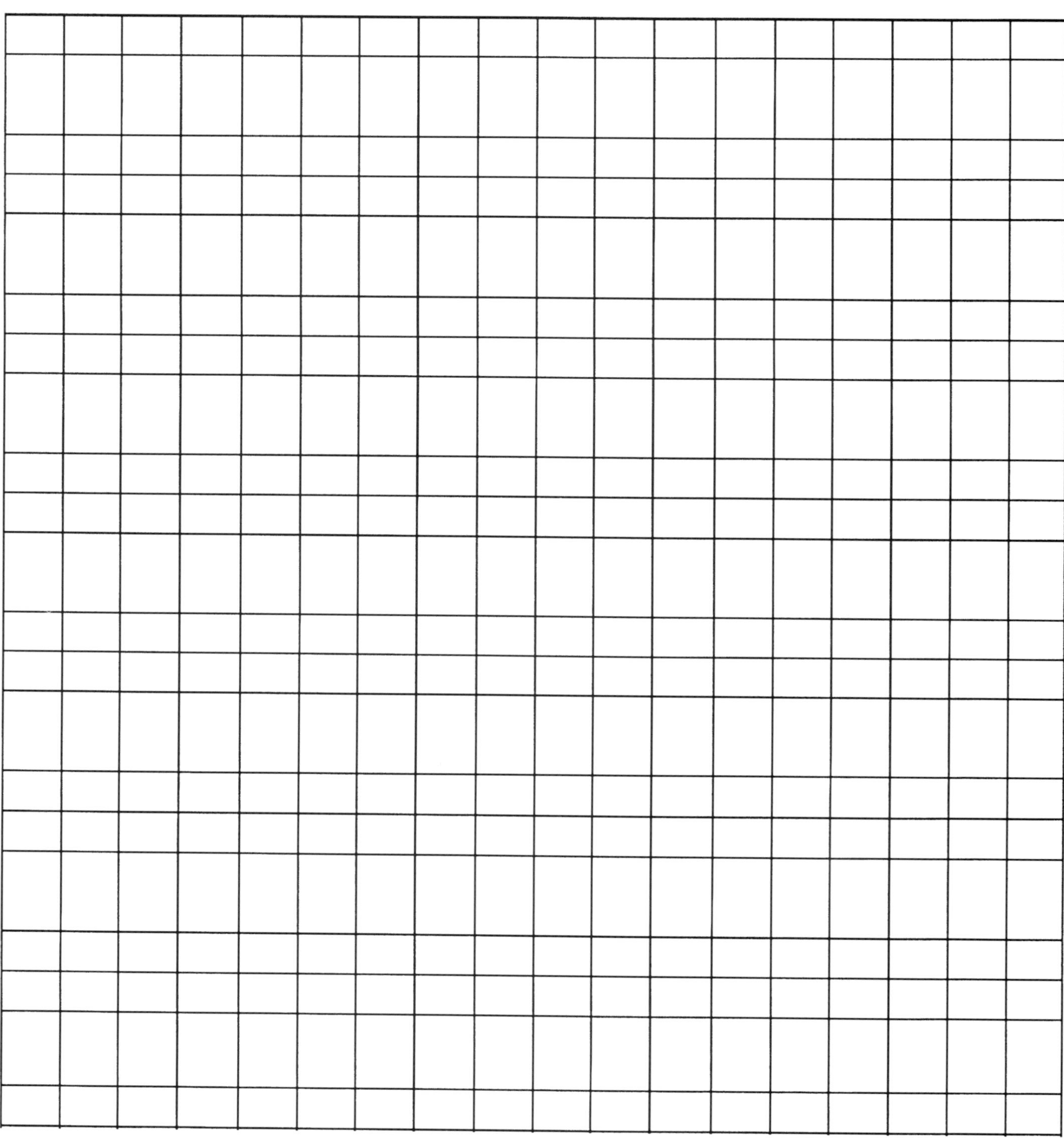

Uncial #2

Wide Fountain Pen (B or B-4), Small Calligraphy Marker (2 mm)

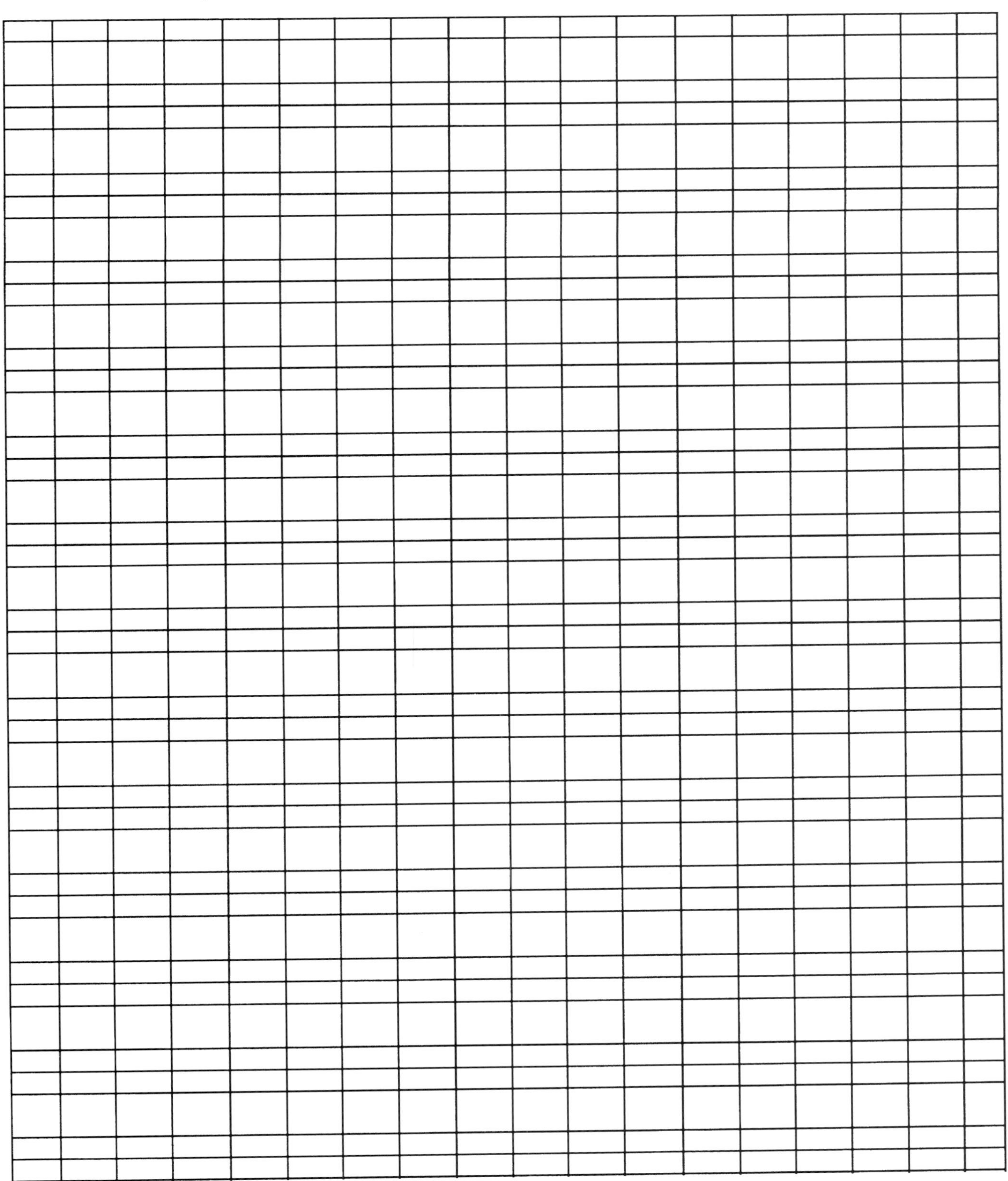

Roman #1

Pointed Marker, Wide Fountain Pen (B or B-4), Small Calligraphy Marker (2 mm)

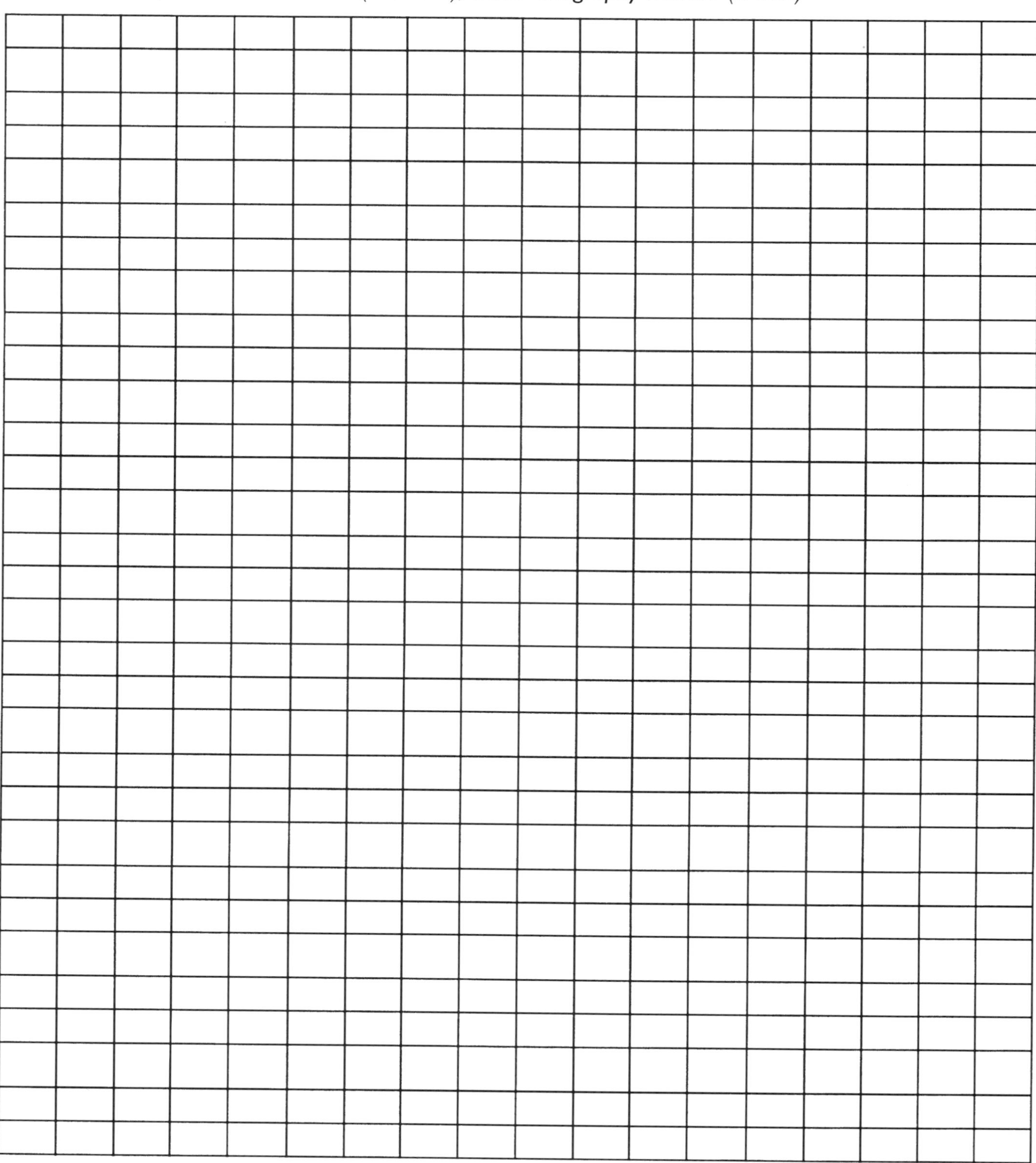

Roman #2

Wide Calligraphy Marker (3.5 mm)

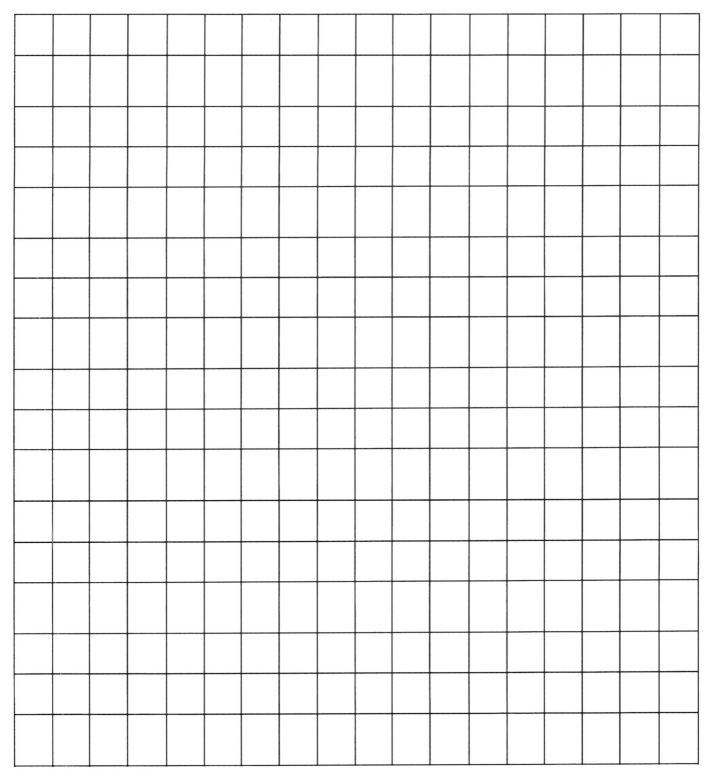

Small Writing (Italic)

Small Fountain Pen (M or B-2)

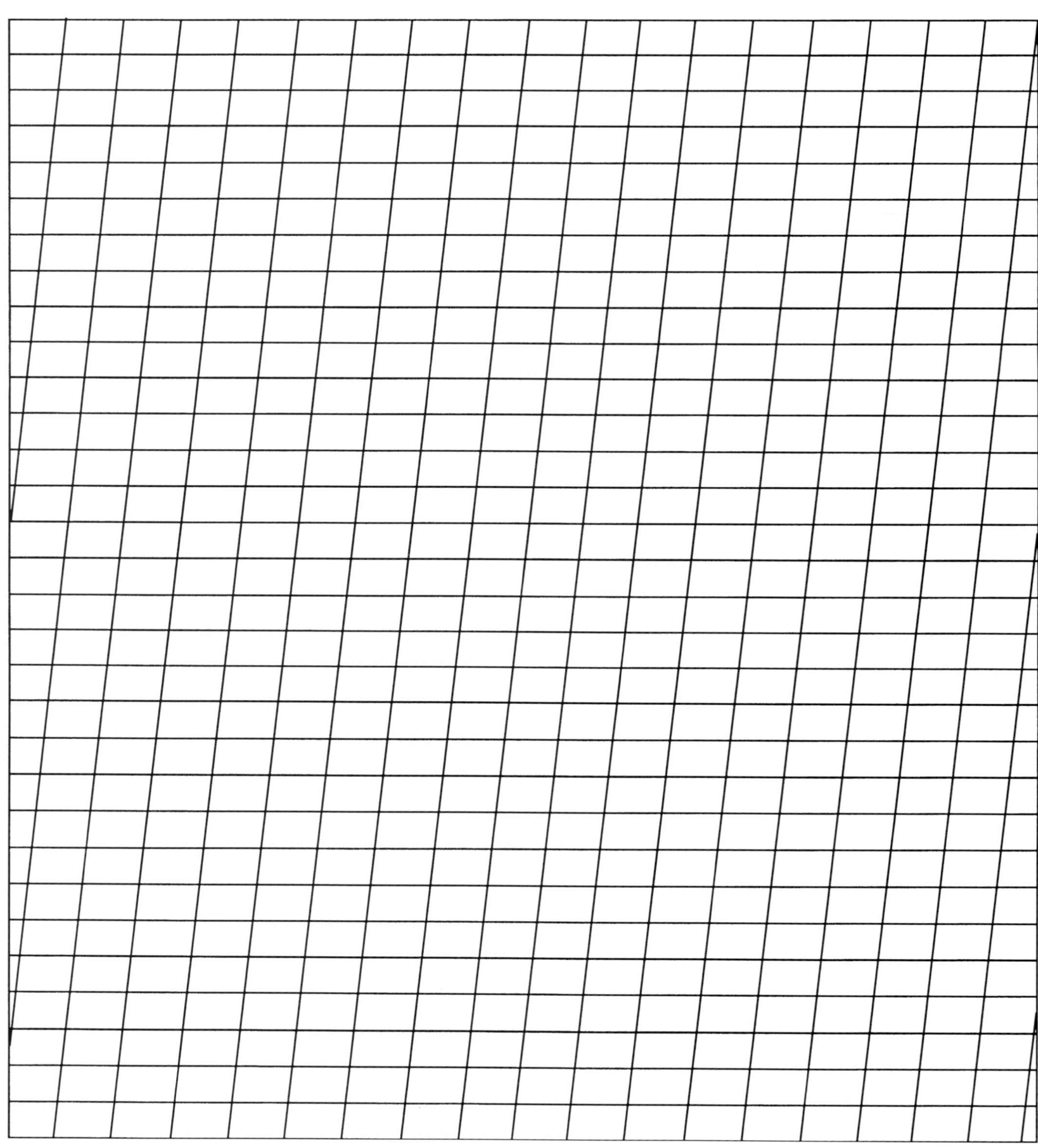

Small Writing

ROMAN

Small Fountain Pen (M or B-2)

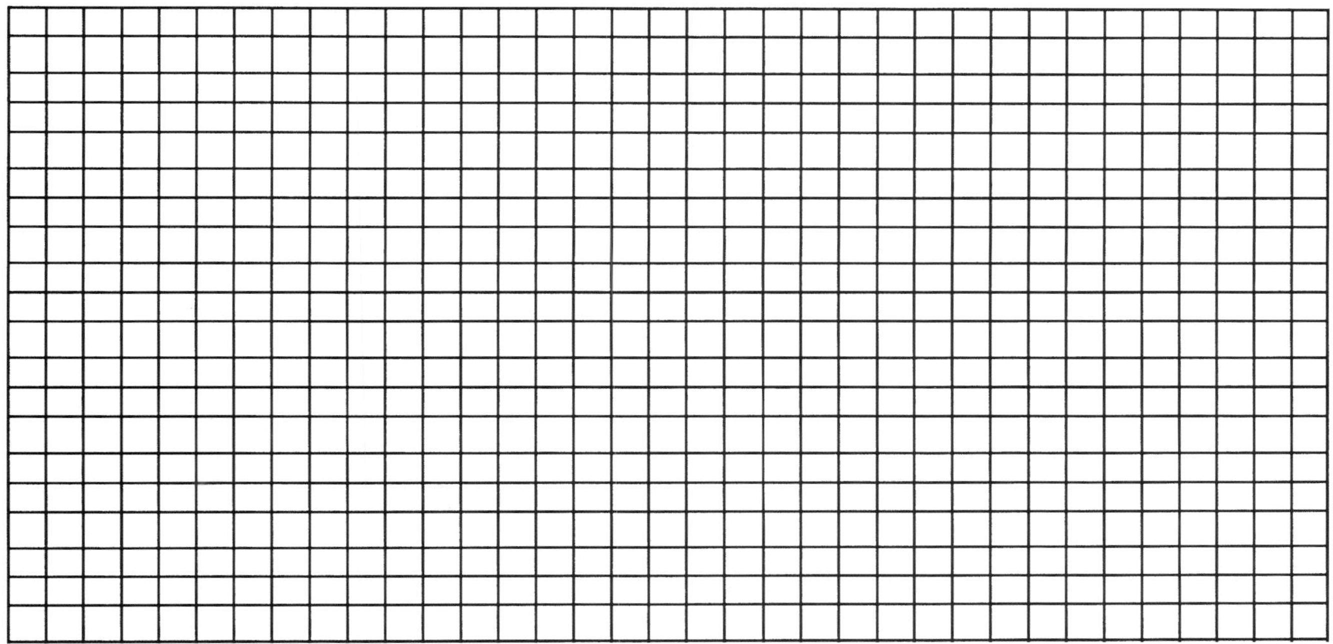

UNCIAL

Small Fountain Pen (M or B-2)

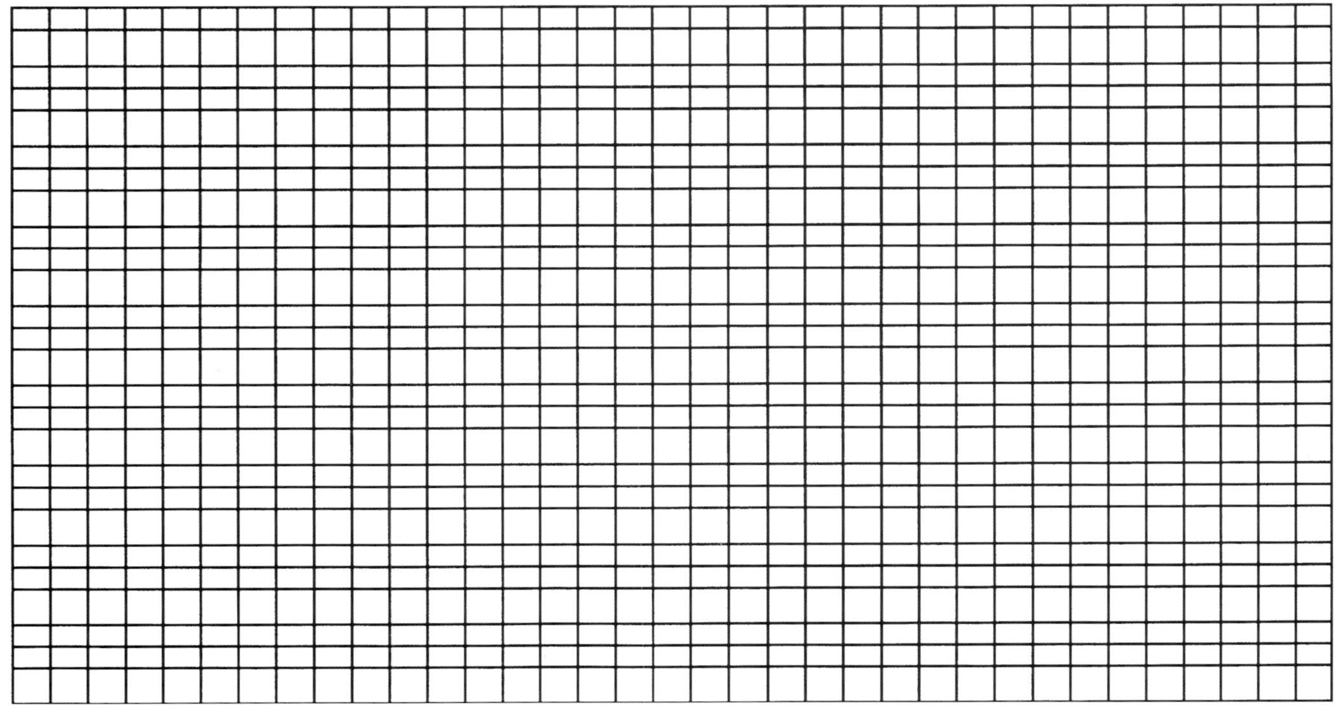

Index

alphabets; see specific calligraphy types
ampersand (&), 90
apostrophes, 90
ascender, 9, 10, 24, 36, 49, 67
ascender line, 9, 10, 57
baseline, 9, 10
basic rules
  Gothic letters, 50, 62
  letter sizes and nibs, 34–35
  lowercase letter parts, 24
  pen position, 21
  spacing, 33, 50
  writing slowly, 44
Black Letter, 48; see also Gothic calligraphy
bookhand, 10
border designs, 96–99
broad-edged fountain pen, 12, 17
  Gothic lowercase letters, 55–56
  italic capital letters, 44
  italic lowercase letters, 34–35
  Roman lowercase letters, 78
  smaller nibs, 92–95
calligraphy, defined, 7, 10
capital letters; see Gothic capital letters; italic capital letters; Roman capital letters
cards; see greeting cards
chisel-edge markers, 11–12
  beginning exercises, 17–18
  Gothic lowercase letters, 49–54
  italic capital letters, 44
  italic lowercase letters, 29–32
  Roman capital letters, 82–85
  Roman lowercase letters, 74–77
colons, 90
commas, 90
counter, 10
crosses, 20, 65
curves, 21
descender, 9, 10, 24, 67
descender line, 9, 10
diagonal pen position (45° angle), 20, 21, 29, 44, 49
downstrokes, 19, 38
entrance strokes, 10, 25
exclamation points, 90
exit strokes, 10, 25
flattened pen position (30° angle), 21, 64, 65, 66, 74
fountain pen; see broad-edged fountain pen
Gothic calligraphy, 48–63
  history, 48–49
  pen position, 49
  Textura style, 49
Gothic capital letters, 57–63
  basic rule, 62
  basic strokes, 58
  beaks and claws, 58
  big-curve letters, 60
  decorative strokes, 58, 61–62
  double-stroke letters, 58–59
  guide lines, 57, 121
  illustrations with, 57
  S, X, and Z, 60–61
  text samples, 63
Gothic lowercase letters, 48–56
  basic strokes, 49–50
  guide lines, 49, 55, 120, 121
  letter exercises, 50–54
  spacing, 50, 55
  text samples, 55–56, 63
  using chisel-edge marker, 49–54
  using fountain pen, 55–56
greeting cards, 100–111
  accordion-fold cards, 105–108
  copy-machine cards, 108–111
  simple folded cards, 100–105
guard sheets, 10, 16, 18
guide lines, 10, 12, 18, 117–27
  erasing, 99
  Gothic capital letters, 57, 121
  Gothic lowercase, 49, 55, 120, 121
  italic capital letters, 38, 44, 118
  italic lowercase, 23, 118
  pen positions, 18, 117
  Roman capital letters, 80, 82, 124, 125, 127
  Roman lowercase, 73, 74, 124, 125, 127
  small writing, 95, 126–127
  Uncial calligraphy, 66, 71, 122–123, 127
hairline, 10
hand, 10, 49
height (italic letters), 34–35, 36, 37
history, of calligraphy, 7, 48–49, 64, 73
holding pencil/paper, 15
horizontal lines, 20, 65
illustrations (illuminated capitals), 57
ink cartridges, 12
invitations, 112–115
italic capital letters, 36–47
  basic facts, 36
  downstrokes, 38
  guide lines, 38, 44, 118, 126
  height, 36, 37
  pen position, 44
  round letters, 42–43
  skeleton forms, 37
  slants, 36, 44
  small writing, 92–95, 126
  spacing, 44
  strokes, 38–40
  swashes (decorative strokes), 36, 40–42
  text samples, 46–47
  using chisel-edge marker, 44
  using fountain pen, 44
  using pencils/pointed markers, 37–44
italic lowercase (minuscule), 23–35
  a-shape family, 26, 30
  b-shape family, 27, 30
  diagonal pen position, 29
  guide lines, 23, 126
  letter families, 25–29
  mistakes, correcting, 31–32
  o and e family, 28, 30
  overview, 23–25
  skeleton forms, 24
  slants, 23
  small writing, 92–95, 126
  spacing, 33–34
  straight-line family, 25
  s, x and z, 28, 30
  using chisel-edge marker, 29–32
  using fountain pen, 34–35
  using pencils/pointed markers, 24–29
  v and w, 28, 30
learning calligraphy, 8, 116
lighting, 16
line exercises, 19–21, 65
lowercase letters
  entrance/exit strokes, 25
  Gothic; see Gothic lowercase letters
  italic; see italic lowercase (minuscule)
  parts of, 24
  Roman; see Roman lowercase (minuscule)
majuscule, 10; see also capital letters
materials, 11–13; see also specific materials
Middle Ages, 7, 57
minuscule, 10; see also lowercase letters
nibs, 10, 12, 92–95
numbers, 87–89
ornaments, Gothic, 61–62
paper, 13, 15
parentheses, 90
party invitations, 112–115
pen angles, 10, 21
  basic exercises, 19–21
  diagonal position (45° angle), 20, 21, 29, 44, 49
  flattened position (30° angle), 21, 64, 65, 66, 74
  Gothic calligraphy, 49
  italic letters, 29, 44
  maintaining, 21
  Roman calligraphy, 74
  Uncial calligraphy, 64, 65
pencils, 13
  holding, 15
  italic letters with, 24–29, 37–44
  Roman calligraphy with, 73–74, 80–81
pens; see also broad-edged fountain pen; chisel-edge markers
  basic exercises, 19–21, 65
  getting to know, 17–21
  positioning; see pen angles
  preparing to use, 18
  smaller nibs, 92–95
periods, 90
posture, 14
practicing, 16; see also specific calligraphy types
preparation, 14–16
  guard sheets, 16, 18
  holding pencil/paper, 15
  lighting, 16
  posture, 14
punctuation, 90
question marks, 90
quill pen, 7
quote marks, 90
Roman calligraphy history, 73
Roman capital letters, 80–86
  extra-wide letters, 85
  groups, 80–81
  guide lines, 80, 82, 124, 125, 127
  medium-size letters, 83
  narrow letters, 84
  pen positions, 82, 85
  round letters, 82
  using chisel-edge marker, 82–85
  using pencils/pointed markers, 80–81
Roman lowercase (minuscule), 73–79
  basic strokes, 74–77
  guide lines, 73, 74, 124, 125, 127
  pen position, 74
  practicing, 78–79
  skeleton forms, 74
  spacing, 78
  using chisel-edge marker, 74–77
  using fountain pen, 78
  using pencils/pointed markers, 73–74
rules; see basic rules
scribes, 7
sitting position, 14
small writing, 92–95, 126–127
spacing, 10
  Gothic lowercase letters, 50, 55
  italic letters, 33–34, 44
  Roman calligraphy, 78
  Uncial calligraphy, 71
straight-line family, 25
strokes, 10; see also specific calligraphy types
swash capitals, 36, 40–42
Textura Gothic style, 49
tools, 11–13; see also specific tools
Uncial calligraphy, 64–72
  basic strokes, 66–71
  guide lines, 66, 71, 122–123, 127
  history, 64
  pen position, 64
  skeleton forms, 66
  spacing, 71
upstrokes, 19
vertical lines, 20, 65
vocabulary, 9–10
waistline, 10
wavy lines, 21
width (italic letters), 34–35
x-height, 9, 10, 24, 36, 49, 67
zigzag exercises, 19–20, 65, 66